Joe Stahlkuppe

Great Danes

Everything About Adoption, Feeding,
Training, Grooming, Health Care, and More

Filled with Full-color Photographs
Illustrations by Michele Earle-Bridges

BARRON'S

CONTENTS

GREAT DANES: AN INTRODUCTION

Taller than the largest wolf that ever lived and possessing a physique that demands attention and respect, the Great Dane is also among the most sensitive of dogs. Powerful enough to knock a large man to the ground and yet gentle enough to nuzzle a sleeping infant without waking the child, the Great Dane is a study in contrasts.

The Size Factor

Throughout this book there will be a recurring theme: "Giant dogs bring giant responsibilities!" It is crucial that any Dane owner or prospective Dane owner understand this. Although ownership of a Great Dane can be immensely pleasurable, ownership of a dog of any giant breed also requires extra thought, planning, and care. The normal situations and circumstances confronting every dog owner are magnified when the dog stands a yard (1 m) high at the shoulder and weighs as much or more than the owner.

Almost every aspect of Great Dane ownership is affected by the size factor. Forgetting this factor in even one instance could have

One of the most regal of all breeds, the Great Dane is also one of the most companionable.

unpleasant or even disastrous consequences. For example, an experienced dog owner purchased a harlequin Great Dane puppy as a pet. The rapidly growing dog was allowed access to both the house and a large doghouse when it was necessary for the Dane to stay outside, as when the owner and his family went away for a weekend. A sudden storm front, rare in that part of the country, plunged temperatures down to 0°F (–17°C). The family returned home to find the young Dane dead, having apparently froze to death. She had grown too large for the doghouse door and her short-haired coat could not protect her from the cold.

Meet the Great Dane

It may seem unnecessary to introduce one of the most recognizable dog breeds in the world, but the Great Dane that many people think

TIP

What's in a Name?

One fact is clear: The Great Dane is in no way Danish! For some reason now lost in the mists of the past, the French naturalist Buffon referred to this breed as the "Grande Danois" or "big Danish" and this name, though rarely used in Europe, was grasped by the English-speaking world.

Ironically, one of the most identifiable breeds in the world still has different names in different places. The Great Dane of England, the United States, Australia, and New Zealand is the "Alano" in Italy, the "Deutsche Dogge" in Germany. While the names are different, the various breed standards remain very similar, all patterned on the German version. The Great Dane then is no Dane at all, but the German national dog that is claimed by the British and misnamed by a Frenchman. Even with all this name confusion, the Great Dane remains one of the most unique and popular giant dogs.

they know may not be the real Great Dane at all! Dane breeders and owners point out that their calf-size pets attract a lot of attention when out in public—on walks, at dog shows, and so forth. People who wouldn't think twice about commenting on a Doberman or a German Shepherd Dog will often approach Dane people with some questions about the dog, its size, how much it eats, and so on. The Great Dane is a real attention-getter.

Sensitivity: What many casual observers do not know is that the huge, perhaps even awe-inspiring, dog has many attributes that make it an unique pet. For example, under the big, tough exterior, Great Danes are often quite sensitive. Some owners report that an unintentionally loud reprimand can cause a Dane to go to a safe area in the home and withdraw for lengthy periods of time.

Danes often lean against their beloved humans and one dog did this with a wobbly toddler, causing her to fall down. The child, who was also learning to talk at about the same time, pulled herself up by grabbing firmly onto the Dane's muzzle, looked the dog straight in the eye, and proceeded in unintelligible baby jabber to berate the careless canine. The child's parents found the deeply chastened Dane in his crate looking very sad indeed. It was hours before the dog would come near the child who had already forgotten the incident.

Malleability: Another Dane trait that may not be widely known is their high degree of malleability. Great Danes can become spoiled, aggressive, or even too passive when humans allow them to become so. Great Danes have done well in obedience work, the show ring, Schutzhund work, and as pets. A cruel owner who habitually mistreats a Dane could get a dangerous dog for his efforts. A lazy owner who will not take control and help a Great Dane become a good pet may get a stubborn dog that tries to dominate its humans. An owner who has obtained a good-quality Great Dane from a reputable source, and planned and prepared and cared for the dog, can reasonably expect to get a super super-sized pet.

Physical Appearance: From a physical standpoint, the Great Dane is almost a contradiction in terms—elegant/strength, artistic/power. Not only is the Great Dane great in height, it is also muscular without the heaviness of the Mastiff, Saint Bernard, or Newfoundland, but with more substance to go with its tallness than the Greyhound or Scottish Deerhound. The Dane has the regal bearing and demeanor that has often been presented in sculpture and paintings.

History of the Breed

We do not know precisely when this breed originated. We do know that dogs resembling Great Danes have been in the company of humans for hundreds of years. While some British breed authorities do not agree, the Great Dane appears to be largely a German creation and one in which Germany takes considerable pride. It is also true that a very similar dog to the Great Dane was evolving in England and that modern Danes probably do owe some debt to these early British dogs in addition to the German contributions to the breed.

The ancestors of the Great Dane were most likely of hunting stock. Since the Dane is a taller, trimmer counterpart to the English Mastiff, it is probably related to the Mastiff in some way. The Dane has even been called the "German Mastiff" in several countries.

Great Danes, in whatever country, were originally hunting dogs, especially for the fearsome and dangerous European wild boars. These boars bore little resemblance to barnyard porkers and were tough and potentially deadly. Hunting boars required a dog of courage, speed, and exceptional power. The early Danes fit this model and succeeded admirably at the task.

The large boarhounds made a logical transition from a purely sporting dog to a protective guard dog. This change took place over many years and required added attributes other than just the ability to hunt boars. Protection dogs had to be more people-oriented, of less violent temperament, and able to do tasks other than hunt boars.

The one-time boarhound first became a guard dog and then a family pet.

Almost from its beginning as a recognized breed, the Great Dane was embraced by the dog breeders and citizens of Germany. So much would the Germans come to admire the Great Dane that it became the "Deutsche Dogge," or the German Mastiff.

The Germans put stringent requirements for the breeding, care, and training of the "Deutsche Dogge." By setting tough rules and by adhering to them, not only did the Dane become a large elegant dog, but also a large, powerful, and useful dog.

The American Kennel Club Standard

General Appearance: The Great Dane combines, in its regal appearance, dignity, strength

German Popularity!

Many well-known Germans owned Great Danes. Notably, Otto von Bismarck loved Great Danes and did what he could to further the breed. One of the most fabled Germans of all time, Manfred von Richthofen, the Red Baron of World War I aviation, owned a Great Dane named Max and would often put the big dog in the second seat of his plane and take the Dane up into the world of early manned flight.

The Great Dane was originally a hunting dog, capable of holding its own with savage boars, wolves, and other animals. These black Danes just enjoy being in an outdoor setting.

and elegance with great size and a powerful, well-formed, smoothly muscled body. It is one of the giant working breeds, but is unique in that its general conformation must be so well balanced that it never appears clumsy, and shall move with a long reach and powerful drive. It is always a unit—the Apollo of dogs. A Great Dane must be spirited, courageous, never timid; always friendly and dependable. This physical and mental combination is the characteristic which gives the Great Dane the majesty possessed by no other breed. It is particularly true of this breed that there is an impression of great masculinity in dogs, as compared to an impression of femininity in bitches. Lack of true Dane breed type, as defined in this standard, is a serious fault.

Size, Proportion, Substance: The male should appear more massive throughout than the bitch, with larger frame and heavier bone. In the ratio between length and height, the Great Dane should be square. In bitches, a somewhat longer body is permissible, providing she is well proportioned to her height. Coarseness or lack of substance are equally undesirable. The male shall not be less than 30 inches at the shoulders, but it is preferable that he be 32 inches or more, providing he is well proportioned to his height. The female shall not be less than 28 inches at the shoulders, but it is preferable that she be 30 inches or more, providing she is well proportioned to her height. Danes under minimum height must be disqualified.

Head: The head shall be rectangular, long, distinguished, expressive, finely chiseled, especially below the eyes. Seen from the side, the Dane's forehead must be sharply set off from the bridge of the nose, (a strongly pronounced stop). The plane of the skull and the plane of the muzzle must be straight and parallel to one another. The skull plane under and to the inner point of the eye must slope without any bony protuberance in a smooth line to a full square jaw with a deep muzzle (fluttering lips are undesirable). The masculinity of the male is very pronounced in structural appearance of the head. The bitch's head is more delicately formed. Seen from the top, the skull should have parallel sides and the bridge of the nose should be as broad as possible. The cheek muscles should not be prominent. The length from the tip of the nose to the center of the stop should be equal to the length from the center of the stop to the rear of the slightly developed occiput. The head should be angular from all sides and should have flat planes with dimensions in proportion to the size of the Dane. Whiskers may be trimmed or left natural.

Eyes shall be medium size, deep set, and dark, with a lively intelligent expression. The eyelids are almond-shaped and relatively tight, with well developed brows. Haws and mongolian eyes are serious faults. In harlequins, the eyes should be dark; light colored eyes, eyes of different colors and walleyes are permitted but not desirable.

Ears shall be high set, medium in size and of moderate thickness, folded forward close to the cheek. The top line of the folded ear should be level with the skull. If cropped, the ear length is in proportion to the size of the head and the ears are carried uniformly erect.

Nose shall be black, except in the blue Dane, where it is a dark blue-black. A black spotted nose is permitted on the harlequin; a pink colored nose is not desirable. A split nose is a disqualification.

Teeth shall be strong, well developed, clean and with full dentition. The incisors of the lower jaw touch very lightly the bottoms of the inner surface of the upper incisors (scissors bite). An undershot jaw is a very serious fault. Overshot or wry bites are serious faults. Even bites, misaligned or crowded incisors are minor faults.

Neck, Topline, Body: The neck shall be firm, high set, well arched, long and muscular. From the nape, it should gradually broaden and flow smoothly into the withers. The neck underline should be clean. Withers shall slope smoothly into a short level back with a broad loin. The chest shall be broad, deep and well muscled. The forechest should be well developed without a pronounced sternum. The brisket extends to the elbow, with well sprung ribs. The body underline should be tightly muscled with a well-defined tuck-up.

The croup should be broad and very slightly sloping. The tail should be set high and smoothly into the croup, but not quite level with the back, a continuation of the spine. The tail should be broad at the base, tapering uniformly down to the hock joint. At rest, the tail should fall straight. When excited or running, it may curve slightly, but never above the level of the back. A ring or hooked tail is a serious fault. A docked tail is a disqualification.

Forequarters: The forequarters, viewed from the side, shall be strong and muscular. The shoulder blade must be strong and sloping, forming, as near as possible, a right angle in its articulation with the upper arm. A line from the upper tip of the shoulder to the back of the elbow joint should be perpendicular. The ligaments and muscles holding the shoulder blade to the rib cage must be well developed, firm and securely attached to prevent loose shoulders. The shoulder blade and the upper arm should be the same length. The elbow should be one-half the distance from the withers to the ground. The strong pasterns should slope slightly. The feet should be round and compact with well-arched toes, neither toeing in, toeing out, nor rolling to the inside or outside. The nails should be short, strong and as dark as possible, except that they may be lighter in harlequins. Dewclaws may or may not be removed.

Hindquarters: The hindquarters shall be strong, broad, muscular and well angulated, with well let down hocks. Seen from the rear, the hock joints appear to be perfectly straight, turned neither toward the inside nor toward the outside. The rear feet should be round and compact, with well-arched toes, neither toeing in nor out. The nails should be short, strong and as dark as possible, except they may be lighter in harlequins. Wolf claws are a serious fault.

Coat: The coat shall be short, thick and clean with a smooth glossy appearance.

Color, Markings and Patterns:

Brindle—The base color shall be yellow gold and always brindled with strong black cross stripes in a chevron pattern. A black mask is preferred. Black should appear on the eye rims and eyebrows, and may appear on the ears and tail tip. The more intensive the base color and the more distinct and even the brindling, the more preferred will be the color. Too much or too little brindling are equally undesirable. White markings at the chest and toes, black-fronted, dirty colored brindles are not desirable.

Fawn—The color shall be yellow gold with a black mask. Black should appear on the eye rims and eyebrows, and may appear on the ears and tail tip. The deep yellow gold must always

be given the preference. White markings at the chest and toes, black-fronted dirty colored fawns are not desirable.

Blue—The color shall be a pure steel blue. White markings at the chest and toes are not desirable.

Black—The color shall be a glossy black. White markings at the chest and toes are not desirable.

Harlequin—Base color shall be pure white with black torn patches irregularly and well distributed over the entire body; a pure white neck is preferred. The black patches should never be large enough to give the appearance of a blanket, nor so small as to give a stippled or dappled effect. Eligible, but less desirable, are a few small gray patches, or a white base with single black hairs showing through, which tend to give a salt and pepper or dirty effect.

Mantle—The color shall be black and white with a solid black blanket extending over the body; black skull with white muzzle; white blaze is optional; whole white collar is preferred; a white chest; white on part or whole of forelegs and hind legs; white tipped black tail. A small white marking in the blanket is acceptable, as is a break in the white collar.

Any variance in color or markings as described above shall be faulted to the extent of the deviation. Any Great Dane which does not fall within the above color classifications must be disqualified.

Gait: The gait denotes strength and power with long, easy strides resulting in no tossing, rolling or bouncing of the topline or body. The backline shall appear level and parallel to the ground. The long reach should strike the ground below the nose while the head is carried forward. The powerful rear drive should be balanced to the reach. As speed increases, there is a natural tendency for the legs to converge toward the centerline of balance beneath the body. There should be no twisting in or out at the elbow or hock joints.

Temperament: The Great Dane must be spirited, courageous, always friendly and dependable, and never timid or aggressive.

Disqualifications:

Danes under minimum height.

Split nose. Docked Tail.

Any color other than those described under "Color, Markings and Patterns."

Approved March 8, 1999
Effective April 28, 1999

The Great Ear Controversy

To crop or not to crop might seem to be the question for the future for some Great Dane enthusiasts. The ear trimming that is done on Great Danes is called cropping and there are strong voices both for and against it.

Originally, when the Great Dane was the boarhound, its ears were cropped to protect it from the tusks of the large wild boars. Later, the aristocratic look of the cropped ears was kept more as an attractive feature than as a hunting precaution.

Ear cropping is still the norm for Great Danes of show quality in the United States, but is not practiced in many other countries. The AKC standard for the breed does not come out against the practice, and gradually, uncropped are becoming more accepted in breed competition. As of right now, the decision about whether your Dane's ears should be cropped rests in your hands.

If you are going to have this cropping done, it should be done at about seven weeks of age by a skilled veterinarian, experienced with cropping, who feels comfortable with the practice. After their ears are cropped, the puppies must be stoutly bandaged and kept from pawing at their still tender ears.

The Blue Merle Controversy

As with the newly accepted mantle Great Dane color pattern, an unaccepted color—blue merle (or just merle) has been a part of harlequin breeding for many years. Blue merles are similar to the harlequin in that they both have ragged black patches as a part of their color pattern.

Where the merle differs from the harlequin is that the merle's base color is blue or bluish while the harlequin's base color is pure white. For many years (and for some breeders even now), merle puppies born into harlequin litters were destroyed. Merles cannot be shown in Dane classes in AKC shows and may be good pets, but they are not to be considered rare or exotic and demand more than basic pet prices.

UNDERSTANDING THE GREAT DANE

To physically understand the Great Dane, one must combine the height of the Irish Wolfhound, the presence of the Mastiff and the athleticism and sweet disposition of the Greyhound. To emotionally understand the Great Dane, one must imagine an overly large young boy possessed of the most tender of hearts. Failing to grasp both the power and the kind spirit of most Danes is to misunderstand the breed entirely.

It is certainly true that the Great Dane possesses impressive size, but size alone is not what makes the Great Dane great. The regal bearing, the expressive face, and dignity of the dog make it memorable along with its grand proportions.

To understand the Great Dane, one must acknowledge that the aggressive nature of the boarhound/guard dog had to be modified into a more placid, yet still watchful demeanor. As the early Great Dane breeders solidified the breed type, they were ever vigilant in trying to produce a giant alert dog that would always be safe around people and other animals.

A contrast in great strength and incredible gentleness, this fawn Great Dane carefully nuzzles a tiny French Bulldog.

Dedicated Dane breeders worked to produce a reliable and temperamentally sound breed. The modern Great Dane is the end result of long years of strict selective breeding. By carefully seeking a Great Dane from stock noted for good temperament and then by following through with adequate training, today's potential Dane owner should find this giant better behaved than many breeds.

The Nature of the Breed

Great Dane breeders often point out that the big dogs are generally quite sensitive. To non-Dane people, the idea that such a huge canine could actually get its feelings hurt by words alone seems humorous at best, if not slightly unbelievable. That a dog weighing over

130 pounds (58.5 kg) would be more sensitive than some of the toy breeds weighing less than 5 pounds (2.25 kg) seems incomprehensible.

Although a sensitive nature definitely does exist for many Great Dane, it would be an error to brand the breed as giant softies or pushovers. A well-trained Great Dane from a good genetic background, in a home setting where the humans involved are knowledgeable and well prepared, can be an excellent pet. Great Danes usually want to love and be loved by their humans and the ones that do best are those that spend the most time with their families.

Great Danes as Family Pets

For the family that wants a really big canine member, and that is willing to take responsibility for a bigger than big dog, the Great Dane can be an excellent addition. For the single person with adequate time to give a Great Dane the care and training it will need, the Dane is also a good choice.

Great Danes exiled to the kennel or to the backyard for days or weeks on end, become kennel and yard dogs whose personalities may not advance much past a big dog out back that eats, sleeps, relieves itself, barks, then starts the cycle all over again. To sentence any dog, especially a Great Dane, to such a life is a subtle but definite form of abuse.

Great Danes can become great family members, knowing their place in the family hierarchy, fitting into most of the family activities. While a large house with a large, fenced yard would be the best situation for any giant dog, Great Danes given adequate training and sufficient exercise have shared condos and apartments

There are six Great Dane colors currently accepted by the AKC: blue, harlequin, fawn, brindle, black, and mantled (formerly referred to as "Boston"). Each of these colors has a strong fan base of breeders and admirers.

with their owners. The degree to which a family or individual has a successful outcome owning a Great Dane is directly proportional to the level of commitment that family or individual is willing to give.

Great Danes in Obedience Work

Great Danes are not seen in obedience trials with the same frequency that one sees German Shepherd Dogs, Golden Retrievers, and some other breeds. A number of Danes have however, done very well in their pursuit of obedience titles.

Obedience trials, licensed by the AKC offer the following titles (which go after the dog's name as in Baron O'Sullivan of Hauppauge, C.D.) for the dogs and owners who are willing to put in the training time to learn an increasingly difficult group of tasks:

Companion Dog (C.D.); Companion Dog Excellent (C.D.X.); and Utility Dog (U.D.) Guidelines on what is required and how to get involved in obedience trials are available from the AKC (see Information, page 92).

While most dogs can certainly be improved with appropriate training, for a dog the size of a Great Dane, training is an essential. In obedience work, as in regular training, the dog must be under the control of a human being and not the other way around. Obedience training a Great Dane can be a very rewarding experience, but also possibly a frustrating one. Not every dog, including every Great Dane (or every Great Dane owner), is a good candidate for the discipline and hard work required to be successful in obedience work.

Great Danes as Show Dogs

One famous breeder/exhibitor of harlequin Great Danes once suggested, "Perhaps one reason that this breed does so well in the show ring may be because Great Danes are always on exhibition in one form or another." Danes do seem to attract a lot of attention, even when they are just out for a walk with their owners. Even at dog shows where Great Danes are often seen, a really excellent specimen will attract the attention of viewers who would never classify themselves as Great Dane enthusiasts or perhaps not even Dane fans! Perhaps it is the combination of size, structure, power, and elegance that captivates onlookers.

Great Danes as Guard Dogs

The Great Dane is an impressive guard dog if it simply stands still and barks. It is as a deterrent that the Great Dane does its best work as a guard dog. Certainly some do reasonably well in guard dog training. As a breed, Danes just don't seem to relish such work the way Dobermans, Rottweilers, and some others do. That Danes are not as often seen in the Schutzhund competitions where trained dogs attack well-padded "enemies" is probably viewed as a real positive by the people who wear the pads. Great Danes may not love guard and attack work like some breeds do, but when motivated to attack, a Great Dane can be an awesome, intimidating force.

If you want a live-in pet that will give its life to protect you, a Great Dane is a good choice. If you want an attack dog solely for the purpose of serving as a guard, do yourself and an innocent Great Dane a favor—choose another breed!

LIVING WITH A GREAT DANE

One Dane owner assessed the size factor of living with a Great Dane as: driving a large bus through city traffic; an adult trying to exist with furniture designed for pre-schoolers and getting in and out of the shower with the girth of Orson Welles. Size is the predominating aspect of living with a Great Dane. This aspect can't and won't be ignored.

"Great" Means More than Just "Big"

An adult Great Dane is much larger than a German Shepherd Dog, or a Collie, or even a Rottweiller, all breeds appropriately thought of as "big" dogs. At maturity, most Great Danes will be able to easily put their chins on the surface of the average dining room or kitchen table.

The length of the average Dane's body when full grown will exceed, when the tail is included, the height of most adult human males. Such a long body requires sufficient turning and maneuvering space in a home, in a kennel,

Like this handsome black dog in this awesome setting, living with the Great Dane requires living life on a larger-than-large scale.

in a run, or a yard. The weight of the average adult Great Dane will be as much as that of most teenagers and many adult humans. A large Great Dane can actually occupy much more space on a couch—if it is allowed to be on a couch—than two average-sized humans.

The Dane's tail is a mighty whip that can in one swish sweep a coffee table clean of China cups or bric-a-brac. It can knock a toddler down with enthusiastic wagging. A Great Dane that jumps up on people—a very bad habit to allow any dog to learn—can topple larger children and smaller adults. The toenails of an excitable Dane puppy can rake furrows across furniture or human skin.

Add to the physical aspects of Dane ownership the fact that these dogs are fond of leaning on people and things whether or not the things or people are capable of withstanding such demonstrative affection. Older people and children need to realize that Danes like to be physically next to the people they love; they have to brace themselves for the onslaught of an adoring dog.

Although these physical aspects would seem to point to making the Dane a purely outside pet, that should not be the case. While Great Danes certainly enjoy some time outside every day, for walks, in a yard, or a kennel run, they adore their humans and will want to be inside with them. The sensitive nature of the Dane will be hurt if it is exiled to an outdoor environment and never allowed to interact with its humans in their home. Sometimes such a dog will strive all the more for attention and to get inside where the people it cares for live.

Great Danes and Children

Great Danes can be excellent companions for children. Some Danes seem to have an innate love for these little humans and other than the accidental spills that a big dog can cause a small child, the two get along well together.

Children are sometimes less reliable than Great Danes in being gentle and kind. After they get over their initial awe at such a huge dog, some children cannot be trusted not to injure even this biggest of dogs. Children must be reminded that this is a dog and not a pony and the dog is not to ridden, kicked, or struck. Very small children or even other not-too-trustworthy older children should always be supervised by an adult when allowed to spend time with a Great Dane.

While Great Danes are normally very good with children, responsible parents should always teach their children that a strange dog is not to be approached until an adult says it is okay to do so. Parents should also instruct their children that there are times when any dog, even a Great Dane, may not be in the mood to be a good playmate. When a dog is eating, when a female has puppies nearby, or when the dog is injured or ill are all times when the dog is best left alone. Overly aggressive dogs should never be allowed to be near children, and overly aggressive children should probably never be allowed near dogs.

Great Danes with Other Dogs

Great Danes are not usually bullies. They don't usually have to be. Their size alone seems to intimidate all but the feistiest dogs. While male Danes are like many males in many breeds, territorial as far as other male dogs are concerned, unless a strange dog is actually intruding on a Dane's space it won't have too much to fear from the big dogs.

Generally, a Great Dane can easily adapt to life with other dogs in the household with no more difficulty than most other breeds. Of course, bringing two strange adult unneutered males into the same household and expecting them to act like playful puppies shows little awareness of dogs and their behavior.

Great Danes with Other Pets

Many Great Dane breeders relate how their Danes not only get along with cats and other family pets, but actually come to be pals with other animals in the home. As with strange dogs and the Great Dane, a good dose of

Make sure all your food is well out of reach—dogs this size have a tendency to get into everything!

preparation laced with common sense is appropriate here. If you bring an adult Great Dane that has never been around small animals into a home setting, there may be some problems. If a Dane puppy is reared with other pets, then it comes to view them as part of the home and generally no problems ensue.

Great Danes and Strangers

Great Danes are not always fond of strangers. These dogs like to know what they will encounter in their environments. A visitor in the home who is accepted by the Dane's owners may be treated with a cool reserve at first. After a person has shown that he or she is no threat to the home or the dog's owner, the stranger may receive a variety of responses, from being benignly ignored to being lavishly adored.

Great Danes that have been thoroughly socialized as youngsters will have no trouble accepting mannerly strangers either in or outside the home. The very size of the Dane alone is enough to discourage strangers from bother-

ing such a dog's owner. Danes can be the gentlest of dogs, but they are still dogs; they don't always understand that a child, another animal, or a stranger doesn't mean them any harm. Part of the responsibility of being a Dane owner is anticipating and eliminating situations or conditions perceived as threatening.

CARING FOR YOUR GREAT DANE

Putting a Great Dane outside for much of its life is akin to sentencing someone to solitary confinement. While a Dane does take up a great deal of space within a home, it is within this home that the dog can come closest to reaching its true potential as a companion animal. Caring for such a dog begins and ends with the amount of time and effort an owner is willing to expend.

Ownership of any dog brings with it certain responsibilities and giant dogs bring giant responsibilities, in the area of general care. Responsible Dane owners will learn what good pet care means and will do their best to see that such care is provided. Great Danes have much to offer as companion dogs, but their care is somewhat different from that needed by some other dog breeds.

Housing a Giant Dog— Inside and Outside

That the space needs for Great Danes are different from those for Schnauzers, Corgis,

A Dane puppy will thrive and grow into magnificent adulthood with lots of attention and human interaction.

or even for Afghan Hounds is understandable and even obvious. Just what those space needs are may be not be as clearly understood. It has been suggested that a prospective Dane owner take a yardstick or a measuring tape around the house and measure potential problem areas so that an adult Great Dane can be kept out of troublesome situations as much as possible. Great Dane height is but one concern; its weight and the length of its body even when on all fours must also be taken into account

The Crate

The best method of allowing a dog to live inside is to provide for it, from its very first night in the home, a cage, crate, or carrier that will be the dog's own special place within the household. (see Crate Training, page 52). The use of a crate as a home-within-the home for a dog makes use of a natural instinctual trait that all dogs, as denning creatures, seem to have. In the wild, canines will be born in and spend a good portion of their lives in and around a lair or den that is thought to represent a place of safety from the outside world.

By using the denning behavior of dogs, humans have been able to not only make dogs, such as the Great Dane feel safer and more comfortable within a house, but have also used this behavior as an aid in training (see Housebreaking, page 51). The crate will be discussed more fully in other sections, but a prospective Great Dane owner should know that the

A kennel or fenced yard designed for the average dog will not keep a giant Dane inside. Even with a good doghouse with a strong and high fence, a Great Dane will want and need to be inside with the humans it adores!

process known as "crate training" is absolutely the best way to keep a Dane within the confines of a human abode!

The Doghouse

Since Great Danes are often both inside and outside dogs, a doghouse within a kennel run or a fenced backyard is also a good idea for this breed. Such a house should be built or purchased with the rapid growth of a Dane in mind. It should also be constructed specifically for the needs of the Dane and not be simply some used shipping box, old chicken coop, or discarded wooden barrel. There are some excellent commercially designed doghouses available. Such a house is very preferable to the average noncarpenters' rendition of a doghouse for a Great Dane. A doghouse should be a warm, dry, draft-free place for the dog to go when it is not with you inside your home.

The Yard

The area around a Dane's outside quarters also deserves some consideration. Giant dogs demand giant responsibility in this area too. A backyard or kennel fence that could keep many smaller breeds securely inside is nothing more than an easy jump for a Great Dane. Most Dane breeders believe that a fence should be at least 6 feet (180 cm) high to keep a giant, athletic dog inside it.

The construction of the fence is also important. Danes are, as mentioned, "leaners." If a 150-pound (68 kg) dog leans on a poorly constructed fence, door, or gate long enough, it may fall. Also, some Danes are great diggers and can somehow squeeze their big bodies *under* some fences that they can't go over.

Exercise and the Great Dane

Great Danes, although very big and athletic dogs, are somewhat calmer than some other breeds. Certainly, a Dane that lives primarily inside needs adequate exercise to keep it healthy. It is also true that an outside dog may not get all the physical activity that it may need for good health just by being in a run or small backyard.

Great Danes must have daily exercise to keep them in good physical and mental shape. This type of exercise can come in the form of regular walks with their owners or other members of their families. The Dane and the human will benefit from being out in a park or in safe walking areas, being together for a special time on a consistent basis, and being able to get all the cardiovascular benefits that come from steady strolling.

Because a Dane weighs 150 pounds (68 kg) and some humans can weigh the same or less, control of the dog must rest on more than physical domination. An out-of-control Chihuahua can be scooped up into the arms of its owner and thus can be kept away from a harmful situation. Not many people will be able to handle a Great Dane in the same way. Always be prepared to avoid potential problems when out on walks with a Dane and try to avoid trusting natural instincts that may tend to make your pet misbehave.

Grooming

Grooming a Great Dane is a good deal easier than many other breeds. Because there is so much more area on a Great Dane, simplified

CHECKLIST

When You're Away

Boarding your Great Dane is a very plausible alternative to the rigors and stresses of extended travel. There are several options for boarding your dog:

1 There are many quality boarding kennels across the country that are accredited with the American Boarding Kennel Association (ABKA) (see Information, page 92); The ABKA teaches its member kennels the best ways to care for its clients' pets. Some boarding kennel owners will possess the coveted CKO, Certified Kennel Operator, designation showing that they have studied their craft and have passed numerous tests.

2 Your Great Dane may be able to stay at home under the care of family, friends, or neighbors.

3 There are also professional pet sitters, who should have references and be bonded, who will take care of your dog.

4 Your Great Dane's veterinarian may have some extra space for your dog at his or her clinic.

5 Under certain circumstances, if your Dane's breeder lives nearby, maybe this person won't mind having a visiting alumnus stay for a few days.

grooming is no small blessing. Keeping the big dog clean and presentable should be no huge task, but there are some points that need to be handled:

A strong line or family of dogs often shows great similarity between its members, as do these three mischievous-looking six-month-old brindle pups.

The end result of many hours of care, training, and providing tangible and intangible life elements all pay off when a puppy matures into the "Apollo of the dog world," the adult Great Dane.

This young uncropped brindle Dane is pensive but calm knowing that its owner is just as close as the other end of the leash.

Wayward ear and all, this young black Dane shows potential of great size and imposing demeanor.

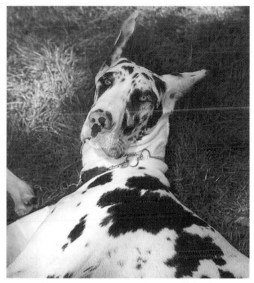

Danes, while large and dignified, can be funny and even puppyish all their lives.

Originally boarhounds, the Dane became, like these two blues, excellent companion and guardian dogs for members of royalty and large land owners.

Showing all the charm of a Great Dane puppy in the newly accepted mantle color, this youngster deserves the best possible home with the best possible owners.

✔ Because the Dane's face is so much a part of the beauty of the animal, make every effort to keep the Dane's ears, eyes, muzzle, and chin clean. These are also areas that are difficult for your dog to clean for itself.

✔ Don't bathe your Dane too often. Too frequent shampooing will make the Dane's coat and skin dry and possibly flaky. If the house dog gets really dirty, then a bath is of course necessary.

✔ Pay close attention to cleaning your Dane's teeth. This is a grooming task best started when the dog is still a puppy.

✔ Feet and toenails need regular inspection. It is very important to keep a Great Dane's nails evenly trimmed—another task best begun in puppyhood—to avoid any foot problems that can be aggravated by the large size and weight of the Dane, (see Feet and Nails, page 87).

✔ Keep watch during your regular inspections for external parasites. Fleas, ticks, and ear mites can make your Great Dane (and you) miserable and possibly spread diseases. Keep these critters away from your pet (see Parasites, page 79).

Providing Tangibles and Intangibles

Caring for your Great Dane should never be allowed to become a chore or an unpleasant job. Your Dane must depend on you for almost everything that impacts on its life. When you become a dog owner, especially when the dog is a Great Dane, you have a real responsibility.

There are many tangible things that you obviously must provide: housing, food and water, medical care. These tangibles are usually recognized and known before you get a dog and they are all part of having a pet.

There are some intangible things that your Great Dane deserves also: your attention, your correction, your affection. Unless you provide these intangibles your Great Dane becomes nothing more than a big, living possession, and unless you provide these intangibles, your Dane becomes merely another of your possessions,

Responsible Dane ownership begins with a clear understanding that though your pet may be regal in bearing, giant in size, sensitive in demeanor, brave in appropriate circumstances and loving in all ways—it is still a dog! As a dog, a Dane must have wise, careful and consistent human leadership in a world fraught with dangers, complexities, and uncertainties.

*This drawing, more or less to scale, will
give you a good idea of the enormity of the
Great Dane as compared to other large dogs.*

albeit a living one. There is nothing worse than a Great Dane being banished from the household because it grew too big and is now relegated to the lonely and frustrating life of a kennel dog that will see its humans only when they come to provide the perfunctory food and water. In such a circumstance a Great Dane is probably better off dead, or certainly away from you and in the hands of someone who will both let the dog express its love and receive your love in return.

A Great Dane puppy placed in your care can become a wonderful pet and companion. It can live with you, anticipating your highs and lows and trying its canine best to share them with you. It will be a watchdog, a nursemaid, a friend, and a noninterrupting listener, but it has to be molded into this great pet and companion. Such a dog will not come about by accident and it will not happen in the hands of a person who really doesn't deeply *care* for the dog, as well as regularly care for the dog.

CONSIDERATIONS BEFORE PURCHASING A GREAT DANE

Ownership of a Great Dane isn't really like ownership of a smaller dog. That the Dane will require more room is clear. That a giant dog may have greater needs than just living space may not be as obvious.

Illusion and Reality

There are many things about the breed that can make a Great Dane a truly special pet in the right home. There are also some aspects of Dane ownership that may be incompatible with your household. Deciding if this breed fits your needs, wishes, and expectations is a task that no Great Dane breeder, no dog authority, or no book can do for you. This decision must be made by you and the other members of your family. Failure to seriously undertake this job may result in some inconvenience for the humans involved with possible tragic results for the dog.

In earlier years merle puppies like this one were destroyed at birth by many harlequin breeders just because of their color. Now many merles and other off-colored Danes find good homes as family pets.

It is sad to say, but the Great Dane often suffers from an inability of the real dog to live up to the vision of the fantasy dog. Some people buy a Great Dane in order to have the biggest, meanest dog in their neighborhood. Others have a mental picture of strolling in the park with a magnificent Dane drawing the admiration and envy of passersby. Still others envision themselves lounging in their book-lined den with a giant canine companion stretched out at their feet.

These fantasies are easy to imagine. Putting reality to these dreams is quite another matter. The person who wants a Dane in order to have "the toughest dog in town" definitely needs rethinking and perhaps therapy. The Great Dane can certainly fill the size part of this pipe dream, and some Danes could conceivably become vicious enough to satisfy any malajusted dog owner, but such behavior runs counter to what a well-bred Dane should be. Forcing a dog to fit a pattern that is alien or negative to its genetic makeup is true cruelty to the animal.

A Great Dane owner can surely look forward to sharing peaceful moments within a home setting. The Dane does have a reasonably low activity level and can be an excellent home companion, but not without adequate preparation and training. Developing a Great Dane into an acceptable member of a household requires caring, knowledgeable, consistent help from the humans in that household. This task will not be accomplished in a split second, like the mental vision version, but will take time and effort.

Remember that, first and foremost, a good Great Dane should be a good pet. It should be compatible with you and your family, with your family circumstances, and with the realistic things you want a pet dog to be or do. One of the most rewarding aspects of dog ownership is to take a young, impressionable pup and shape it into a truly excellent adult dog.

Searching for the Right Dog

Having decided that you and the Great Dane are right for each other, you now have to find just the right Dane for you. This process may take some time and effort on your part. While Great Danes are not rare, the dog or puppy that has just the right temperament, health history, potential, color, sex, age, and so forth may not be easy to locate.

Where to Look

If you have studied the breed at dog shows, you may already know some Great Dane breeders in your area. This is an excellent place to begin your quest. Talk with several of these Dane breeder/exhibitors, ask questions, take notes. Find out their recommendations on where to seek the dog you want.

Breeders: There may be a Great Dane breeders' organization in your city or state. After you have presented yourself as a serious and well-prepared potential Dane owner, most of these breeders should be willing to help you find the dog you are seeking. In fact, these organizations may be the only way you can find exactly what you want. Great Dane breeder/exhibitors generally will know who among their peers has a litter of pups, perhaps an older pet-quality puppy, or even an adult Dane in need of a good home. Because these are the people showing their dogs, this is probably the only way to go about finding a pup with dog show potential.

Clubs: If you have trouble finding a local Great Dane club, contact the national club (see page 92) or the American Kennel Club (also on page 92) for information about well-known Great Dane enthusiasts not too far from you. The American Kennel Club also has an excellent video about Great Danes. An investment in this videotape would probably be a very good idea for any potential Dane owner.

Magazines: There are magazines available that specialize in Great Danes; some are these are listed on page 93. By learning as much as you can about as many Dane breeders as you can, you will be in a much better position to choose the place from which to obtain your Dane.

Internet: You may also find a great deal of information on the Internet. Whether you visit shows, contact breeders, or read magazines or books, always remember that you are looking for the Dane that best fits your family. Don't accept anything other than just such a Great Dane.

Dog shows: In your search for a Great Dane, you must do some clarification of your objectives. Just what do you want this dog to do for you? If you are seeking a show dog, go to dog shows. Talk with the top breeders of Great Danes today and discover if they have the show prospect you're seeking.

Breeders

What Should Be Expected of You?

Great Dane breeders will be more than willing to help a newcomer find a good dog or puppy, but they are serious about their hobby and will generally expect some things from you. They may want evidence that you are serious about wanting to own a Great Dane and want to give it the best of all possible homes. They may also want to know about your experience with other dogs. Is this Dane to be your first dog? You may want to take good care of a Great Dane, but do you really know how to do so?

Some breeders will question your reasons for wanting a Great Dane. Do you want a big, handsome dog to serve as a fashion accessory? Do you want a Great Dane to be an attack dog? Do you want a Dane because your neighbors got a big dog and you want an even bigger one? Be prepared for this type of quizzing and recognize that a large majority of the Dane people only want to make certain that a puppy doesn't end up in abusive, neglectful, or ignorant hands.

What Should You Expect?

When you approach a Great Dane breeder about a puppy or an older dog, you should expect honest answers from a knowledgeable source. Try to find a breeder whose good reputation is as important as the producing of good Great Danes.

You should generally expect to pay several hundred dollars for a pet-quality and perhaps several thousand for a top show prospect Great Dane. Beware of bargains. The dog-owning world is full of people who, to save some money, took a lesser-quality puppy than they really wanted. Some Dane buyers choose to buy their pups from sources other than reputable breeders and soon discover that the bargain puppy becomes the most expensive pet they have ever owned.

In a breed where the potential for health problems is admittedly higher than in some others, you *must* seek out the best-quality Great Dane possible. Newspaper ads and other sources may advertise a Dane puppy "with all the papers." One now well-known breeder who bought her first Dane from such a source stated, "I discovered that the only papers I actually ever saw for this puppy were the ones on the floor of the room it was in." Your Great Dane is not only a financial investment, but a canine friend that will share your home and life for hopefully a decade or more. Can you afford to buy a close companion animal without having as much documentation and information about it as possible?

Papers

Prior to actually selecting a puppy from any source, make certain that the Dane you may buy has these vital documents and necessary records:

Health records: Current health records showing all vaccinations with dates, wormings with dates, and examinations by a licensed veterinarian, including the results and treatments.

All puppies are appealing, as are these young fawns, but cute, little puppies grow up. Always choose a pet with the adult dog in mind.

This boldly-marked harlequin is the product of many years of selective breeding. Harlequin is a difficult color to produce and is best left to expert breeders.

There are great Great Danes in each of the accepted color as this excellent uncropped blue dog shows.

The black Great Dane is one of the most impressive dogs of any color in any breed.

Great Danes will be reserved and aloof with most strangers, size and appearance alone delivering a powerful deterrent message.

The old adage about always seeing a pup's parents before you buy it is true. You can gauge a lot about how your puppy will look and behave by closely observing its mother (and father, if possible).

Pedigree: An accurate pedigree showing the puppy's parentage and family tree. (The Great Dane Club of America has some strong recommendations about what colors of Danes should be mated together. Be sure that your potential pup's pedigree shows that these color-breeding recommendations have been followed.) This pedigree should also show the champions or obedience title holders in your prospective pup's ancestry.

AKC registration: The AKC registration certificate that confirms that this Great Dane puppy is purebred with its mother (dam) and father (sire) both being registered Great Danes. You should also receive application forms to forward to the AKC in order to register this puppy, if you do buy it, in your name.

CHD Screening: You will want documented evidence that the parents of this puppy are free from Canine Hip Dysplasia (CHD, Hip Dysplasia), (see page 78). While this does not ensure that their offspring will not become dysplastic, the tests, which are performed after a dog is two years old are the best screening techniques currently avaliable.

If you can't get this paperwork, you should *not* buy the puppy. Never accept a puppy on the proviso that "the papers are in the mail." Most Dane breeders are honest, but a puppy is a very important purchase that requires wise business practices on your part.

Most of all you should expect that your study and careful search for a Great Dane with whom to share your life will result in a healthy, temperamentally sound puppy without any genetic defects or inherited physical problems. Your entire experience as a novice Great Dane owner will certainly be affected by your ability to be a knowledgeable, assertive, and careful consumer.

Guarantees—from Both Sides

Most responsible Great Dane breeders will give you a written health and temperament guarantee for any puppy they sell. This guarantee

---

TIP

Christmas Puppies

Contrary to the various advertisements that show the joy on a child's face when it gets a pup for Christmas, Christmas puppies are not a good idea. Bringing a new puppy into the happy chaos of Christmas morning is both unfair and unwise. The puppy has probably never been away from its mother and littermates before and it suddenly finds itself in the middle of people shouting with glee, tearing open packages, and concerned with everything except the well-being of a frightened or bewildered young Great Dane.

✔ Your new family member deserves to be the center of attention, to have its needs met, to be helped in adjusting to this strange new world. Unless the puppy is the only gift your family exchanges this holiday, let the puppy come well before or well after Christmas.

✔ One idea that has some real merit is to buy the AKC videotape about Great Danes and books about the breed and wrap these as gifts under the tree. Then you have not only given the family something to build anticipation for a puppy, but good information that will prove useful later.

should be in writing and should specify that the dog's inherited health and temperament is guaranteed for the life of the animal. Breeders who are confident of the quality of their dogs are the best places to seek your Great Dane puppy.

Reputable breeders will usually have some requirements for you as well. Since many Great Dane breeders take the dogs they sell as a life-long responsibility, they may have some agreements for you to sign:

Spaying or neutering: One such agreement involves your commitment to have spayed or neutered a pet-quality dog or puppy, in order to keep an inferior specimen from producing inferior puppies. This does not imply that this dog or puppy has any physical or temperamental shortcomings, merely that its color may not be just right or some other minor cosmetic flaw is in evidence. Some breeders make a practice of withholding the registration papers until the dog or puppy buyer brings proof from a veterinarian that the animal has been spayed or neutered.

Returning the puppy: Other Great Dane breeders will want to be certain you know that they maintain a strong original ownership interest in the Dane you are buying. If you cannot keep the dog or puppy, the breeder will probably want you to agree to return it rather than passing the animal on to someone else or to the humane society. This for-life concern by a breeder is another sign that you have come to a good place to look for a dog or puppy.

A Puppy or an Older Dog?

The choice here is largely determined by what you want in a Great Dane. If you have had considerable success as a dog owner and merely want a companion, there may be an adult Great Dane, perhaps from a rescue group or shelter, that could move right in and become your best friend. Some adults and older puppies just don't work out with their initial buyers. In other cases, circumstances may necessitate the return of the Dane to the breeder. Quite often these Great Danes readily can adapt to your home and lifestyle. Other dogs, however have picked up bad habits or made attachments to their former owners that may be hard to break.

If you take your time in the choice of an adult Great Dane, you may find just the perfect dog for you and your family. You may be able to help retrain or readapt a maladjusted adult, but this may not have been the purpose of your search initially.

Puppies require a lot of time and effort to become the kind of pet you are seeking. A novice dog owner should probably choose a puppy and let the youngster grow up with the family as the family learns how to train and care for the pet. As adaptable as some older Danes can be, a puppy learns the lessons it is taught usually for the very first time. No retraining or restructuring is required with a youngster that will know only what you taught it.

Male or Female?

Your expectations for your pet will also influence your decision about the gender of your pet. Male Great Danes are larger than females and they possess a masculine bearing and presence that one sees in most males. Males will be more territorial than females, and perhaps more likely to attempt escape from the backyard in order to "cruise" the neighborhood.

above left: This fawn puppy will need the right environment and the right care if it is to fully reach its genetic potential.

above: This is sure to be one of the safest cars in town!

left: The Great Dane has made the transition from ferocious hunter to brave protector, to loving canine companion.

These Danes appear to be almost a part of the mountains that surround them. Their giant size is readily observable. What some people fail to realize is that the Great Dane is also one of the most incredible canine athletes in the world; size with strength, power with speed.

Although they tower over males and females of most other breeds, female Great Danes, should be decidedly feminine in their graceful and elegant appearance. They are somewhat less aloof with strangers and other dogs than are males. Since unspayed females go into heat with the estrous cycle about every six months and have to be safeguarded at these times to prevent unwanted litters, owning a female has its own set of concerns.

A properly trained, well bred Great Dane of either sex should be an excellent pet for the right family. If you don't have any serious aspirations as a Great Dane breeder, then either sex with the male being neutered or the female being spayed should prove right for you.

Pet Quality or Show Quality?

A pet-quality Great Dane is not less healthy, less temperamentally sound, or—other than cosmetically—less a Great Dane than a show-quality dog. A show-quality Dane should also not sacrifice health or temperament in order to be a show dog. Both categories of Great Dane should be able to become excellent companion animals. Without that, you don't want either of them!

If the show ring is your goal, buy a puppy "with show potential." In the experienced eye of a Great Dane breeder, this puppy with such potential looks like other puppies that went on to become successful show dogs. Puppies change a great deal as they mature. Although many show-potential puppies live up to a breeder's expectations, others don't and are then relegated back into the pet-quality ranks. In a common practice, one Dane breeder took

a pick-of-litter puppy back as a stud fee payment and the young bitch progressed well until the breeder noticed a possibly inheritable defect that ended the show and breeding career for this Dane. The once top-pick puppy became a lovely spayed pet for a family that adores her.

Because truly great show dogs are rare in any breed, a puppy with show potential is significantly more expensive than a puppy already identified as a pet prospect. Furthermore, as a novice in Great Danes and in the show ring you have little chance of being allowed a really top-flight show puppy unless you agree to provide the puppy every chance to achieve its show ring potential.

Choosing a Puppy

By this time you and your family have decided what you want in a Great Dane puppy. You have given the matter considerable thought and study. You have assessed your household's capacity to provide a good home for a Great Dane. You have visited a number of dog shows and have seen what really good Great Danes look like. You have talked with and perhaps even visited with, some Dane breeders, seen their dogs and their homes. You have puppy-proofed your home (see page 42), and had a high fence erected around the backyard. You now seem ready to choose a puppy.

Several breeders near your home have litters of pups in the color that you like. You have decided that a healthy, pet-quality female puppy with a good disposition is just what you want. You recognize that there is enough demand, even for pet pups, that the price may be several hundred dollars.

When picking up a gangly Dane pup, always support the pup's rear end with one hand while holding it comfortably under the chest with the other hand.

When you visit these breeders you ask to look at only the female pet prospects. This simplifies your choice and you don't have to become attracted to a show-potential pup only to be told that it doesn't fit your pup profile. Take time to observe the puppies; watch how they interact with each other and with their mother. Carefully handle each puppy, paying attention to the ones that seem alert, unafraid, and well adjusted. After you have carefully looked at each pup, ask the breeder about the puppy that you like best.

Commit to buying a puppy only after *your* veterinarian has examined it and found it to be healthy and free from serious defects, including temperament Then, and only then, have you found your new canine family member.

How to Pick Up a Puppy Correctly

Even as youngsters, Great Dane puppies are not exactly small.

✔ When picking up a gangly, full-of-fun Dane puppy, always support its rear end with one hand.

✔ Hold the youngster comfortably under the chest with the other hand. In this way, you can look at a puppy without danger of it jumping or falling from your grasp.

BRINGING YOUR GREAT DANE HOME

The first contacts between you and your Great Dane are crucial to the future of your relationship. Carefully choreograph your first contacts and your early moments with this young giant. Bad habits (on the part of both human and canine) have a way of getting worse—much worse.

The Initial Phases

If you have visited your puppy several times at the breeder's, you have already begun the bonding process that will make a specific puppy and a specific owner a team. The bonding process with your dog, combined with early socialization with other humans, cannot be overestimated in its significance in helping your puppy grow to be the best-adjusted adult possible. Remember that being well adjusted takes on added importance when a dog is as large as a Great Dane.

Getting to know your new puppy while it is still at the breeder's is usually a good idea. If a few brief visits and playtime with the puppy, without its dam or siblings present, are possible, your Dane will be leaving home with friends instead of strangers. Even this brief introduction to you can certainly help your puppy. This

Inviting a giant dog into your home will involve some adjustments, for you and for the dog.

bonding period may not be necessary or possible with every pup, but if the opportunity to ease yourself and your family into the young dog's life presents itself, by all means take it.

The trip home: The use of a crate/cage/carrier for travel with your Dane is always recommended when transporting a canine by automobile. Be sure to have a couple of old towels to put in the carrier or in case the pup suffers from motion sickness.

If your initial trip home with the puppy is a long one—several hours or more—be sure to plan rest and relief breaks at least once each hour. Even though your Dane is still a relatively small puppy, you *must* be sure that you have a collar and leash on the dog whenever it is out on these breaks—a puppy can get into harm's way before most humans can react. Prevention, in the form of a good collar and leash and an alert attitude, could save your new pet's life even before it gets to its new home.

Early training: When you arrive home, even before you take the puppy inside, take it *immediately* to a preselected urination and defecation spot. You may want to "salt the mine" by dropping some litter from the puppy's first home that has urine and/or feces scent on. This will encourage the pup in learning that this site is where such activities are to be done. Remember that this first relief time is very important; stay with the pup in this location until it relieves itself and then enthusiastically praise it for doing the right thing at the right place at the right time. Then you can go inside and introduce your pup to your home.

Puppy-proofing Measures

You most certainly should have puppy-proofed the areas to which the youngster will have access. Puppy-proofing means that you have removed from these places everything that could do harm to an innocent, ignorant, and inquisitive puppy. Some of these things are

✔ Tight squeezes—behind a stove or upright piano or between banister railings, where a puppy could get trapped or caught.

✔ Heavy items on tables that could tip over or fall on a puppy.

✔ Stairwells, patios, porches, open windows that could lead to a possible fatal fall.

✔ Access to common items such as household cleaners, air fresheners, poisonous houseplants, antifreeze, and exposed wiring or extension cords that could kill your dog if ingested or chewed.

✔ Small, easy-to-swallow things that could harm your pet such as tacks, pins, rubber erasers, and children's toys.

✔ Doors and gates to the outside that a quick puppy could dart through or get caught behind and injured.

These are just some of the items and situations that you will need to eliminate or barricade for the safety of your puppy. If your puppy has access to a garage or driveway, every family member needs to be certain that the young dog is absolutely safe (with another person or in its carrier or kennel) *before* a car is moved. Many pets are killed by autos driven by their owners.

Great Danes grow rapidly. The tabletop that was secure from a curious Dane puppy two months ago, may be right within reach now. Do a complete puppy-proofing job the first time and update your efforts every week or so as the young giant matures.

Adjustment Time

When your puppy first comes to your home, its new home, there should be an adjustment time when the puppy is given the affection, caring, and early lessons that will help it quickly fit into your household.

A responsible person, probably an adult or older teenager, should spend enough time with the pup to help it understand some of what is happening in its young life. Much of what the puppy encounters now will be mystifying and bewildering. Until the recent memories of its old family—its mother and littermates—begin to fade, this pup needs support from its new family.

It is natural to want to show the Great Dane puppy off to anyone and everyone, but give the puppy a little time to get to know you and the other members of your household before you spring a whole group of new people on it. Many things are new for this puppy and the more interruption from the regular pattern of life in the family, the longer it will take for the pup to adjust.

The Doggy Den—a Plus and a Must

What does your cute new Great Dane puppy share with the tiny Pomeranian and the wild-running timber wolf? Other than some common ancestry, they share the fact that they, like all canines, are denning creatures. In the wild and right through to your new puppy, canines prefer to have some safe haven to retreat to when things get stressful or perhaps just to rest. This den or lair that is the birthplace of most wild canines has been suitably replaced by a carrier/cage/crate for many house dogs. It will give your puppy a home-within-the-home, a place to go that is uniquely its own place of refuge, sleeping quarters, and sometimes mobile transport to the veterinarian and on trips. Use of such a den device will greatly aid you in helping your puppy settle in. The den will also be an invaluable help in housebreaking the puppy (see Housebreaking, page 51).

Some humans will view this carrier as a little prison for detaining the puppy, but dogs see their dens as an area where they can relax or go when tired or bewildered. Don't let mistaken human views about the carrier cause you and your Dane to miss benefiting from its use of instinctual denning behavior (see Crate Training, page 52).

Helping Your Puppy Settle In—the Right Way

Your Great Dane may be just a young puppy, but it is at its learning peak. The lessons it is taught now, the impressions it gets now, can stay with the dog for the rest of its life. It is your role as human leader and puppy owner to see that your pup gets the right lessons and the right impressions. In the absence of your guidance a puppy may jump to the wrong conclusions about what it is supposed to do and about what it is allowed to do.

The trip home inside a noisy machine with strangers may have been certainly puzzling and perhaps even frightening to an eight- or nine-week old puppy.

Hopefully you have already begun to teach your pup the right place, outside to urinate and defecate. Whoever is in charge of the puppy's adjustment period should try to get the puppy outside to the relief place on as timely a basis as possible. Certainly no noses are rubbed in urine and no physical punishment is meted out to an ignorant pup for making a mess (see Housebreaking, page 51). If given the right training in a consistent fashion most Great Dane puppies can understand where they can and can't go. (With no lessons or the wrong approach, some dogs may *never* learn.)

Sleeping arrangements: By using the crate as a resting place for the puppy and its regular place for it to be when not with you, the puppy already has a place to run to if it gets tired of playing or if it feels unsure or afraid. Your puppy will now have to adjust to being alone without its mother or littermates. In some ways, its new family can replace the old, but this should *not* happen with regard to sleeping arrangements. It may be cute to let a young puppy sleep with you, but how cute will that be with a 150-pound (68 kg) adult dog? Let the puppy sleep in its carrier. You'll be happier and so will the dog.

Now is a time when the entire family must pull together and do what is best for the puppy.

The Great Dane should never be allowed to become totally an outside dog. A close human companion (which the Dane will crave) makes the Dane much happier and a much better pet.

Beginning with the first night in the new home, no matter how much pitiful puppy wailing or how much human hand-wringing there may be, the puppy sleeps in its carrier, *period*. Everyone in the family needs to know that this is best for the puppy and while, like an inoculation, it may appear to hurt, it is really much better for the Dane in the long run.

When the puppy is placed in the carrier for the first night it will naturally be lonely, a little frightened, and anxious to have its new humans come and comfort it. Don't you do it and don't you allow anyone else in the family to do it! No matter how much you paid for this puppy, a weak moment now could turn a potentially excellent companion into a neurotic that has learned that when it wants attention, all it has to do is whimper and cry. This is not a good lesson for your dog to learn and one that may be very hard to unteach!

No one enjoys the prospect of a lonely puppy whimpering itself to sleep for the first few nights in its new home, but unless you want that whimpering to become a reinforced behavior, you must be firm. The puppy must learn that there is a time for interaction with its family and a time for quiet and sleep. A sad, lonely, crying puppy can become a sad, lonely, crying adult if someone in your household

Though they do well inside, Danes also thrive with some exposure to the outdoors.

Danes, though elegant and beautiful should never be allowed to become just another fashion accessory to be trotted out to impress friends and neighbors.

gives in and takes the puppy out of its special sleeping place and cuddles it every time it cries. Steel your resolve and that of your family with the knowledge that your puppy, if left alone, will not continue to cry much beyond the first few days. Consistency now will be a great aid in helping the puppy reach its potential as a good family companion.

Danes, like all dogs should never be allowed to run free in the neighborhood.

There are some things that you can do to help make the puppy's settling-in ordeal somewhat easier.

✔ Use an old-fashioned hot water bottle—the rubber kind with no leaks to mess up the pup's bedroom/den. Wrap it in a towel. This will give the pup a sense of warmth somewhat like its mother.

✔ Perhaps something from the pup's first home that has retained comforting scents could be placed in the carrier to provide it with a little "home" scent.

✔ Some people use an old wind-up alarm clock (non-electric, with the alarm deactivated, for sure) so that its ticking can somewhat simulate the beating of the mother's heart.

✔ Place a radio near (not in) the carrier and turn it on low volume on an all-night talk radio station that gives the puppy some sense of not being alone.

Foods

Other aids in helping your puppy settle in involve feeding the same food it has been eating before it came to you (see Feeding Your Great Dane, page 65). Changing foods now can only add to the physical trauma of its move to a new home. It is also a good idea to feed the puppy on the same schedule it was on at the breeder's. Regulating when the puppy eats is also a good way to project when it will need to go the relief place outside.

Exercise

Don't let your new Great Dane puppy overexert itself. Playing with the pup is fine, but this is still a very young puppy that can play hard only in short spurts. When the puppy appears to be tiring, take it to the crate for a little rest. This tends to reinforce the idea of just what the pup should do in its den.

Remember that this is a Great Dane puppy. Don't expect anything but puppy behavior out of it. These

Have the mother Dane's owner give her a thorough wiping down with a couple of old towels. The towels, full of the mother's scent, can be used to line the new pup's crate and give a "scents" of home, and ease adjustment.

initial days are for first lessons and adjustment, and for settling in. If you take things slowly with the pup now, you'll have a stable foundation on which to build the other training that will come in a few months.

New Puppy Adjustment Tips

✔ Take a plastic baggy with you when you go to pick up the puppy to retrieve a small amount of puppy waste material and litter. This material will aid in "salting the mine" at the new pup's outside relief area.

✔ Go easy on visitors and trips within the first few days the pup is in its new home. Give the youngster a chance to become acclimated to its new surroundings before adding new people and new settings.

✔ Establish a schedule with your baby Dane and try to adhere to consistency. By setting standards (built around the puppy's needs) you will not only help the young dog adjust to its new family, but also assist the family in adjusting to the new pet.

✔ Introduce any pre-existing pets to the new Dane gradually. The last thing your pup needs is to be scolded by an old housecat or dominated immediately by an older dog.

✔ Closely monitor the appearance of the pup and alert your veterinarian to any persistent sneezing, diarrhea, or other possible illness indicators.

✔ Always keep your Dane in its crate at night. Keeping the pup confined at night is not cruel. It is wise. Many young dogs have gotten into serious (sometimes fatal) trouble wandering through a home at night while its owners slept.

✔ Look to the needs of your new puppy as late as possible at night and as early as possible in the morning. Forgetting about a youngster

Never, ever let a Dane puppy sleep in bed with a human. Behavior considered cute in a puppy may be quite different when a giant adult dog wants to do the same thing.

that needs a trip outside can leave you with a messy crate and a messy puppy.

✔ Encourage guests in your home not to interrupt or interfere with the lessons that your Dane pup is learning. Food from a guest's plate is still a forbidden practice. Allowing a puppy on the couch is still not allowed. Explain politely, but firmly, that the rules are for the good of the young Dane and even well intentioned inconsistencies now will only confuse the youngster.

✔ Special safeguards are appropriate for an inexperienced young dog in the case of unusual activities taking place in or around the home. Parties, home repairs and other out of the ordinary events can frighten a puppy or even put its life in jeopardy if someone leaves a door or gate open. Always plan ahead for the comfort and safety of your Great Dane.

TRAINING YOUR GREAT DANE

There is nothing more disconcerting in dog owner-ship than a pet that will not obey. Just seeing a dog hurtling at top speed toward a dangerous or potential disastrous situation, oblivious to the plaintive calls and quasi-commands of its owner is extremely negative. When the disobedient dog in question is a 3-foot-high Great Dane, the word "negative" becomes very understated.

Should You Own an Untrained Dane?

It is foolish to own an untrained dog of any breed, but the height of folly is to possess a dog that you could not possibly physically restrain in emergency situations. The Great Dane that will weigh as much as or more than its owner must be under the control of a human in every possible circumstance. Some control measures are high fences, stout kennels, and strong leashes attached to strong collars—but the best control of all is adequate training.

Your Great Dane may be a wonderful companion, a member of your family, a real canine friend and protector, but the best Dane in the

Danes are sensitive, often clownish and full of fun. These attributes are always enhanced when dogs of this breed are the recipients of good training. An untrained Dane is a definite liability.

world is still just a dog. Dogs will usually react to situations in doglike ways. A bitch in season in the neighborhood can turn the calmest Great Dane into a hormonally charged Romeo. If your dog will not obey your call to come to you at a time like this, then your dog is not fully trained and could present a danger to itself or others.

Training your Great Dane gives you an opportunity to build into the dog some restraints, some ingrained habits, some specific behavior that you can control. Without this control you have a giant problem animal that could easily get into serious trouble. Protect yourself and protect your dog; *train it!*

Using Pack Behavior to Simplify Training

Your Great Dane is a pack animal. All dog packs have a leader and social hierarchy in which each individual animal knows exactly

What Dog Training Is All About

Getting your Great Dane to do what you want it to do is not cruel and isn't just some control game that you can use to show your friends and neighbors how you can manipulate a huge dog. Training your dog is as much for you and the members of your family as it is for the dog.

✔ Before you can teach a dog anything, you have to decide what you want it to learn. You also have to decide on a "lesson plan" on how you will handle those things you wish to teach. By becoming even an amateur dog trainer, you will become a much better dog owner.

✔ You will have to understand what your dog can learn before you can train it. By doing this you will have to become more acquainted with the learning needs of the dog.

✔ If approached correctly and in the right frame of mind, training your dog will help it become a much better pet and companion and can very well be one of the most rewarding parts of pet ownership.

✔ While you may go on to teach your Great Dane a wide variety of cute, even amazing tricks, your first priority is to teach the dog things it needs to know to be a better functioning pet.

its own place. Puppies are taught pack behavior by their mothers before they ever leave the whelping box. Pack behavior is just as significant for your Great Dane as it is for any wolf living in the wild. By understanding pack behavior you can use it to help you train your dog.

The "Alpha Male" Concept

Pack leadership always involves the strongest animal. In dogs and wolves this leadership position is generally held by an adult male in his prime with sufficient life experiences to guide the pack in the business of day-to-day survival. Because size and strength play a key part in this concept, and male canines are usually larger and more powerful than their female counterparts, the leader of the pack is called the first or "alpha" male.

In the wild, the alpha male gets the best of the food, his choice of breeding-age females (usually known as the "alpha female"), and his will is law in the pack. The alpha male zealously protects his pack from other canines and will kill or banish any contender to the throne. The alpha male remains so only so long as he is the smartest and strongest.

You, your family, and your Great Dane make up a pack. You or some family member will have to assume alpha male responsibilities and hopefully the hierarchy will have each human at a point above the Great Dane. You as alpha male will have to be stronger than the Dane. Installing yourself in this role usually comes much more easily when your Dane is still a puppy. It is possible to become the boss of an adult Great Dane, but if that adult has itself been in the top spot, a stubborn clash of wills could result.

Because "nature hates a vacuum," if you or some other person in your family fails to become alpha male, your Dane may try this position for itself. When this happens, the proverbial cart is truly before the horse-sized dog. Unless you can reassert your leadership and move the dog down several notches in the "pecking order" you may have a difficult if not potentially dangerous situation. Imagine that you have a 150-pound (68 kg) canine tyrant in your home, one that will do only what *he* wants to do.

Failure by the human members of a household to take firm control have resulted in more than one potentially good Great Dane ending its life as an unwanted pet at the dog pound, or as a vicious dog chained to a stake in a junkyard. Don't let this unnecessary tragedy happen to your dog. Just as children need a clear understanding of the rules of the family and the lines of authority supporting those rules, so does your dog, whether that dog is a 10-pounder (4.5 kg) or whether it is ten times as large.

When to Begin Training

Some training was begun for you by your Dane's mother. She instilled in her puppies some early lessons while the pups were still unweaned babies. Her example as a dog trainer is a good one for you to follow in the further training of her son or daughter. The training methods used by the mother Dane were

Repetition: Some behaviors were absolutely not to be tolerated and behaving in this way will bring instant correction.

Consistency: Bad behavior was corrected the same way each time. The mother didn't punish a particular act one time and reward it or ignore it the next time, which can only confuse a puppy.

Timeliness: Correction for bad behavior happened immediately, while the offending act could be associated with the resultant negative outcome in the young, impressionable puppy's

mind. (Never did the mother Dane save up punishment and then unload on a youngster long after the sin has been forgotten by the pup.

Fairness: The correction was fair and not overly severe. The mother dog will not normally do a puppy any real physical harm for a youthful indiscretion. A snarl or a rough nudge from Mama, is all that most pups will need to get the general idea that they did something wrong.

As long as the puppies were under her control, these lessons were enforced. The mother didn't count on the pups remembering from one week to the next week what was wrong last week. By repetition, consistency, timeliness, and fairness she taught her puppies their first lessons, which tend to stay with dogs for their entire lives.

If you will follow this canine course in dog training, your job will be much easier, will fit itself into a pattern that most Danes already understand, and thus will have more of a binding effect on the behavior of the dog. Repetition, consistency, timeliness, and fairness worked for the mother and it will work for you!

Housebreaking

Your Great Dane puppy started learning this important lesson on the first day you brought it home. When you immediately took the puppy to the specially designated spot for it to relieve itself and then enthusiastically petted and praised it when it did, you started housebreaking your puppy. Your puppy needed to defecate or urinate and when it did so, at the place you chose, it was rewarded.

Housebreaking for a Great Dane puppy need not be the arduous activity that it has been made out to be. If your puppy does not make a mess inside it will please you, and your puppy

---

TIP

Bladder Control

No matter how much your Great Dane puppy may want to please you, until this puppy is between four and six months of age it will have limited bladder control. Don't expect perfection until the pup matures physically enough to be able to wait to relieve itself. But this is certainly not intended to suggest that you wait six months to begin housebreaking. You need to have the mental lesson firmly in place when the pup's physical functioning reaches maturity.

wants to please you. At this early part of your relationship your puppy and you are in complete agreement. Now your part of the housebreaking task is to help your puppy continue to please you by not making a mess inside. The best way to do this is to understand some basic canine instinctual behavior and to use this behavior to help you help your puppy learn this lesson.

Crate Training

Crate training is the very best and easiest way to help your dog become housebroken. It takes advantage of a side effect of denning behavior. In the wild, animals rarely foul their dens; to do so would be self-defeating. Not only would a den be a messy, smelly place to live, but other predators could more easily find it by following the smell of built-up urine and feces. It is for this reason that dogs, by nature, do not like to mess up their carrier/den (see Crate Training Suggestions, page 54).

Crate training takes advantage of the dog's innate desire to keep its den clean, but it does require a regular plan for puppy feeding and then subsequent trips outside to the relief place. When crate training is used along with a feeding/relief trip plan and you add to this a lot of praise when the puppy does what you want it to do, housebreaking becomes much simpler.

Puppy Physiology

Some understanding on your part of puppy physiology is important. Knowing when your puppy will normally need to relieve itself

Your Dane's entire environment, inside, outside, and when traveling, should be one of safety and security for the dog. Good fences make good pets.

Premium food and lots of fresh, clean water are the fuels that will be needed to develop and sustain any dog, but especially a giant dog like the Great Dane.

Obedience training involves attention and effort from the trainer and from the Great Dane, but a well trained dog makes it all worthwhile.

allows you to establish a regular schedule of going outside. Here are some suggestions about how to time trips outside:

✔ Take the puppy out to relieve itself after it eats or drinks as the additional food or water in the pup's system causes additional pressures on the bladder and colon.

✔ Take the puppy outside the first thing each morning *immediately after* it is released from the crate.

✔ Take the puppy out after it naps during the day.

✔ Take the puppy out after a long and lively play period.

✔ Take the puppy out as late at night as possible.

✔ Take the puppy out immediately if it shows signs of wanting to defecate or urinate, such as staying near the door, circling, sniffing, and looking generally uneasy.

Sometimes you will get the puppy outside just in time. When the puppy relieves itself at the right place, elaborately praise it immediately. Stay right with the puppy until it does eliminate and until it has received its customary award of praise from you. This helps identify relieving itself with the sights and smells of this particular place and with the reward it can expect for doing the right thing. *Never,* for any reason, scold the dog at this special spot! This is where it expects to do its business and then be rewarded. If you scare or punish the pup at this place, it may become confused from the mixed message you are sending.

CHECKLIST

Crate Training Suggestions

✔ Have a positive attitude about cages/crates/carriers and the effective use of instinctual canine behavior in these serving as a den for your Great Dane.

✔ When you buy your first crate or carrier, buy it large enough for the puppy to use as an adult also. To keep the crate from being segmented by the puppy into a sleeping area and relief area (much like the paper training room), make a sturdy partition to keep the den no larger than the puppy requires and then make the space bigger as the pup grows.

✔ Place the den in an out-of-the-way, but not isolated place in the home. Be sure that the crate is not in a direct draft or in the sun or the puppy will not be comfortable.

✔ Put the Dane puppy in the crate for rest periods or when you have to leave the dog unattended for a couple of hours. Upon your return, immediately take the pup out to the relief spot, praise its activity there and come right back in. If you want to go out and play, do so after the break is over so the dog will not confuse elimination with exercise or play.

✔ Do NOT give enthusiastic praise or petting to the pup for about ten minutes after you let it out of the carrier to be with you in the home. Such praise may confuse the puppy and may make it seem that getting out of the carrier is to be rewarded.

✔ Use a stern, tough alpha voice to quiet any crying or whining when the pup is placed back into the carrier.

✔ Keep a mat or old towel in the den along with a favorite toy or durable chew in the crate to keep the puppy occupied when it isn't sleeping.

✔ Never feed or water your Dane in its crate. The place for these things is outside the denning area.

✔ Your family and friends will need to understand the importance of the crate to your Dane pup's overall development, Don't let any member of the household upset the regimen that the puppy will become accustomed to after a few weeks.

Correction

If a puppy defecates or urinates inside, never strike it. A firm, alpha male-voiced *"No"* will let the puppy that this was not good behavior. Never make matters worse by rubbing the puppy's nose in any urine or excrement. Such an illogical action will do absolutely nothing to help the pup learn and may possibly cause it to fear you and leave you with a messy puppy to clean up after.

Feeding

By feeding your Great Dane at regular times you can usually anticipate when the puppy will need to go outside. If you are using a highly digestible, premium puppy food, the pup's stools should be much firmer with much less volume. This aids colon retention and, if an error is made, the mess isn't as bad to clean up. In addition *never* feed a puppy table scraps, even in small amounts. This habit can upset a puppy's system and alter the balance of a quality food. Feed the puppy about three times a day, but don't leave food out continuously as you will have no way of knowing exactly when the pup ate.

Paper Training

While crate training is certainly the best form of housebreaking, it may not work very well for people who can't help the pup get adjusted to the regular schedule of feeding combined with crate training. For those people who have to leave the puppy in a laundry room or a bathroom for the adjustment period, a second, perhaps not quite as effective method for housebreaking is available. This is called paper training.

Paper training involves the confining of a puppy to some easily cleaned room such as a bathroom, kitchen, or laundry room. It does not work particularly well with outside training because the puppy is given two "right" places to go, but paper training may be necessary for those people who cannot constantly stay with the puppy in the first days. Paper training also works fairly well for people who live in apartments where getting a puppy outside quickly may not be easily achieved.

Three basic areas are needed within the room established for the pup's use when you are not with it: a den area (where the puppy's carrier can be placed), a water and food area, and an elimination area. The elimination area should be covered with several layers of newspaper. The puppy will be encouraged to relieve itself on the papers. If observed, the puppy should receive appropriate praise for going on the papers. Since most dogs don't like to soil their food and water area any more than they want to mess up their den, the elimination area needs to be some distance away from the eating and sleeping places.

By using layers of newspapers, urine and excrement can be removed and disposed of by simply lifting the top couple of layers. The puppy's scent will remain and this scent, just as it worked outside, will give the puppy an idea of what it is to do here.

Paper training usually takes a little longer in housebreaking a puppy. Even with paper training, be sure to walk the puppy early each morning and late each night and after meals when you can. Since your schedule prevents you from being with the puppy every time that nature calls, the paper training method is only a stop-gap way of helping your puppy until it has matured more in bladder and colon control.

Just as you might have used some old litter from the puppy's first home to "prime the pump" when teaching the puppy to eliminate outside at the special spot, you can use the same trick to encourage the use of a certain section of the puppy's room. One way to gradually move the pup as it grows from using a paper to using the outside site is to gradually decrease the size of the elimination area and then gradually transport the entire process outside.

If your puppy has an accident somewhere it is not supposed to use, get that area cleaned up as soon as possible. Use an odor-neutralizing cleaner to get rid of the pup's scent; if a smell lingers, the puppy may logically assume that this too is an acceptable site in which to relieve itself.

If you live in an urban area and your puppy must be walked on city streets and sidewalks *always* pick up and dispose of any excreta. Not only is this a responsible thing to do, it is usually the law!

Obedience Training

When to Start Training

A distinction is to be made between housebreaking, settling in, and other early lessons that your Great Dane puppy must know and the more formal training that should not take place before the youngster is around six months old. Though some dogs are ready a little earlier or a little later, at this age the Dane pup should be mature enough to actually gain something out of basic

The Great Dane as a breed is no accident, for hundreds of years were spent building this exceptional canine. The right Dane for you will be no accident either and will require much time in caring and training.

obedience training. *You* are the key in basic obedience training. You must be consistent, confident, and patient if the commands you want to teach are to be learned. Training is not a family function until all the five basic commands (*"Sit," "Stay," "Heel," "Down,"* and *"Come"*) are thoroughly learned. One person must do the training and the training should be done the same way each time.

Training Equipment

Training collar: As equipment for training your Dane you will need a chain training collar

Though two Danes may live in the same home, training should be done separately to keep the dogs focused on the lessons. Each dog must have the opportunity to bond with its humans, be socialized, trained, and given ample personal attention.

(often mistakenly called a "choke chain"). This type of collar is both humane and effective when correctly and appropriately used. This chain collar, which is to be worn only during training session, does not choke the dog. The collar, when correcting pressure is applied, causes the dog's head to come up with a slight snap. This is to get the dog's attention and when applied with the stern *"No,"* this combination not only controls and corrects, but the *"No"* lets the pup know that its action was not what it should have been.

The chain collar should be large enough to go over your Dane puppy's head at its widest part with no more than 1 inch (2.5 cm) of extra room. This collar *must* be removed after training and replaced with a regular collar that can have identification and rabies vaccination tags attached. To leave on the training collar not only fails to make use of the dog's recognizing what is going to happen when this collar is put on it, but if an unattended dog should happen to snag such a collar on something strangulation could occur when the frightened puppy tries to escape.

Leash: With the training collar you will need a 1-inch (2.5 cm) wide leash (sometimes called a lead) measuring 6 feet (1.8 m) long. This leash, which is not to be used on your regular walks with the dog, should be made of leather, nylon, or woven web and it should have a sturdy but comfortable hand loop on one end. On the other end of the leash should be a securely attached swivel snap for attaching to the ring on the chain training collar.

Let your Dane puppy become thoroughly familiar with the chain training collar and the training leash. The dog must not fear these training aids if they are to work effectively. Let the puppy gradually get the weight and feel of both on its neck several days before you actually plan to begin training.

The Five Key Commands

Before you begin to teach your pup, you need to teach yourself how to give commands effectively;

✔ Issue clear, one-word commands to your dog. Use the dog's name before each command as in *"Don, sit."* Be authoritarian in your tone; no place here for baby talk or endearments. You can play with the pup later; right now you should be about the business of training!

✔ Use the same tone of voice each time so that your pup will know by the intonation as well as by your words that you mean business.

✔ Don't confuse the dog by issuing several commands at one time, as in, *"Don, come here and sit down."* Each command has a single, specific word and that word should be used each time and in the same tone of voice.

✔ Remember the canine learning rules and use them:

1. Praise enthusiastically.
2. Correct fairly and immediately.
3. Practice consistent repetition.
4. Never, never lose your temper.
5. Be patient.

Patience

Don't try to take your pup out for a training session when you are angry about something else. The puppy will be able to hear the underlying hostility in your voice and may think that it is to be punished. Training works on a correction/praise system with no place for punitive measures. Wait until you are less emotionally charged before you go out to work with the Dane puppy.

Keep lessons short, no more than 20 minutes. Stick to one new command at a time. Your pup will be doing well to learn all these commands over a period of months. Don't try to build Rome in a day. When the training session is over don't immediately begin playing and roughhousing with your Great Dane; let 20 minutes go by to separate training time with the human with the authoritarian voice from the playtime with the friend.

Note: Other members of the household need to understand that the training of the puppy is serious business. They also need to understand the basics of what you are doing with the pup, so that they will not inadvertently undo your training when they play with the dog.

Sit

The *sit* is a good command on which to start your Great Dane as it already knows how to sit down. Now all you need to do is to teach it when and where to do so.

With the training collar attached to the training leash, place your puppy on your left side next to your left leg, while holding the leash in your right hand. In one continuous, gentle motion pull the pup's head up as you push its hindquarters down with your left hand giving the firm command, *"Sit,"* as you do so.

When the pup is in the sitting position, lavishly praise it. Using the concept of continuous repetition, repeat this lesson until the puppy sits down without having its rear end pushed downward. Remember to keep the same upward

In one continuous, gentle motion, pull the pup's head up as you push its hindquarters down with your other hand, giving the firm verbal command of "Sit" as you do so.

pull on the lead to keep the *sit* from becoming a belly flop. If the puppy shifts in position left or right, use your left hand to gently, but firmly move it back in line. Keep doing this lesson until your Great Dane associates the word *"Sit"* and your firm tone with the lavish praise it will receive if it simply sits down. Soon the puppy will sit upon hearing the command alone without either the rear end downward push or the upward pull of its head. After each successful *sit* praise the puppy liberally and make the praise and what it had to do to get it stick out in your puppy's memory.

Again, always keep training sessions brief. To begin with don't leave the youngster in the sitting position long enough for it to get bored with just sitting there. Gradually increase the time for sitting and always using consistent repetition and the praise reward to help your puppy learn. Several brief, consistent sessions will be much more effective than one long one.

Stay

Do not attempt to teach the *stay* until your Dane puppy has thoroughly learned the *sit.* The *stay* is begun from the *sit* and without that foundation, the *stay* cannot be mastered.

To begin the *stay* command, place your dog in the regular sitting position on your left. Keep some pressure on the lead in your right hand to keep your pup's head up. Giving the clear, authoritarian command, *"Stay,"* step away from the dog (moving your right foot first). At the same time, bring the palm of your left hand down in front of your Dane's face. Your command, the stepping away (always starting on the right foot), and the hand signal *must* be done at exactly the same time and in exactly the same way each time.

Maintain eye contact with your dog and repeat the *stay* command in the same firm tone as before. Do this several times, but don't expect

Show dogs (and their handlers) have to be well trained in order to show their conformation qualities. A poorly trained or unruly dog has no chance in the show ring.

long *stays* at first. Praise the puppy for its *stays,* but if it moves toward you, calmly take it back to the starting point, make it sit, and begin again with consistent repetition of the *stay* command. If the puppy seems to have trouble with *stays,* don't tire it out doing this command over and over and over again. Your puppy naturally wants to be with you, an impulse that this *stay* business stifles. At the end of each short session, if your puppy hasn't yet caught on to the *stay,* finish up with a few *sits* with a good reward for each one and thus end the training time on a positive note. Be patient with your Great Dane, it *will* learn the *stay.*

Giving the clear, firm command of "Stay," step away from the Dane, using your right foot first. At the same time, bring the palm of your left hand down in front of the pup's face.

When the puppy does handle the *stay* command, praise it enthusiastically. Soon you will be able to gradually move farther away and the puppy will understand it should not move. Introduce the release word *"Okay"* in a cheerful, happy tone when you want the puppy to stop staying and to return to you for its reward.

What appears to be a resting Dane is really a well trained agility dog waiting at the end of the dog walk ramp, just as it is supposed to do.

Heel

Once the puppy has mastered the *sit* and the *stay* and feels comfortable with the training collar and leash, you can begin to teach the *heel*. Begin the *heel* command with your Great Dane, in the *sit* position on your left with the pup's head in line with your left foot. Holding the training leash in your right hand and leading off with your left foot, step forward while saying in your firm voice, *"Heel."* As with the other commands use the pup's name to begin the command, as in, *"Don, heel."*

If the puppy doesn't move out with you when you do, pop the leash loudly against the side of your leg and repeat the command, walking away as you do. When the puppy gets the idea and catches up with you, praise it, but keep moving forward. Continue the praise and encouragement as long as your Dane stays with you in the proper alignment.

When you stop, give the command to sit. When your Great Dane becomes comfortable with heeling, it will learn to sit on its own when you stop. Don't let the dog run ahead or lag behind or swivel around to face you. The purpose of the *heel* command is not just to walk with your dog, but to position the dog on your left and teach it to move and stop moving when you move and stop moving. The ultimate goal of teaching the *heel* command is to get your Great Dane to heel without the use of the leash.

Never drag your puppy around just to cover some ground. If your pup has trouble with the *heel* go back to the *sit* and start again. The *heel* may be hard for some dogs to learn, but continue your use of consistent tugs on the leash to keep your Dane moving and keep its head in line with your left leg. Your dog will, through consistent repetition, correction, and reward, learn to heel.

Holding the training leash in your right hand and leading off with your left foot, step forward by calling the dog by name and firmly saying "Heel."

Down

Down begins with the *sit* and the *stay*. Using the lead in an opposite movement from the upward pull of the *sit* and *stay*, pull down on the lead with your right hand, presenting the palm of your left hand with a downward motion while giving the strong command, *"Down."* If the dog is reluctant to lie down as you want it to do, run the lead under your left foot and pull up on it gently, which will force to dog's head down. Remember to repeat both the hand signal and the voice command in exactly the same way each time.

Once the puppy is in the *down* position, pour on the praise. You can help your pup in the beginning by using your left hand much in the way you do to teach the sit, only instead of pushing down on the hindquarters, you will push down on the back while pulling on the lead to make the dog go down on its stomach. It is the downward direction that this command emphasizes, but it should also be used with the *stay*. The ultimate goal is to cause the puppy to go straight down on its stomach on your command and to remain there until released by an *"Okay"* from you.

The *down* can be a very useful and potentially important command for your young Dane to learn. It can be used to stop the dog in its tracks when it might be headed toward some danger. Continue to practice the *down* with the *sit* and *stay* and be certain to thoroughly reward the dog with lavish praise when it stays put in the *down* position. By the use of patience and consistent repetition, you should be able to gradually increase the length of the *down* and even expect to leave your dog's line of sight and expect it to remain in place.

Come

The *come* command may seem both obvious and easy, but there are several important elements to it. Your enthusiasm and use of the dog's name while giving the command, *"Come,"* with your arms held out wide will assure your puppy that you really want it to come to you.

Always use lots of praise on the puppy even though it is doing something it wants to do. Use the training leash and give the dog little tugs if it does come directly to you in a straight line. The *come* is another command that you will want to have obeyed immediately, not after the dog has had a chance to mark a post or watch a butterfly. Treat the *come* like other commands and use your authoritarian voice and the pup's name. Danes can sometimes be a little stubborn or inattentive, but the command with the gentle but firm tugs on the lead should help your Dane pup master this task. After the pup has mastered coming to you from the end of the 6-foot leash (1.8 m) you can switch to a longer one—up to 20 feet (6 m) to reinforce the command that *"come"* means to come from any distance, not just a few feet away. Always reward the dog with liberal petting and praise when it comes to you.

The *come* command is somewhat different from the other basic obedience commands. It does not have to be repeated over and over again in a session. Also, you can unexpectedly use the *come* in play sessions or just when the dog is walking in the backyard. However, you should always expect an immediate response from the dog as it should always expect a reward of praise from you.

Never make the mistake that so many dog owners do and call your dog to come to you and then scold or punish it for some action! This is a form of anti-training. It actually teaches the dog that, "sometimes when I go to the Boss I get punished," and puts some doubt in the dog's mind about whether a reward or a reprimand will be the outcome of coming to you. If a dog needs to be corrected for something, *go to the dog* and do it; don't mess up the dog's natural impulse to want to come to you!

The Importance of Obedience Lessons

If you have never trained a dog before, you may discover that a dog training class may help you and your young Great Dane get more accomplished. Not only are these classes taught by experts who can help you help your dog learn, but this also gives you a chance to spend some away-from-home time with your dog around other dogs and their owners. If your pup shows any inclination toward aggressiveness or toward being stubborn, training classes, which are held several times a year in communities all over the country, may be just what you need to get your dog headed in the right behavioral direction. Ask the breeder where you got the puppy for any recommendations about different classes or teachers. You could find that such a class would not only be helpful, but a lot of fun!

FEEDING YOUR GREAT DANE

Great Danes require careful feeding. The requirements of their great size gained so rapidly, are just the start of the feeding difficulties of this giant breed. Continued care in feeding your Dane is a necessity, not just a nicety. The length of life and the quality of that length of life will depend to a marked degree on what your pet is fed, and how it is fed.

The Importance of a Balanced Diet

All dogs need and deserve food that will meet their nutritional needs, that they enjoy eating, and that can be offered in consistent and convenient ways. Diet is especially important for giant dogs like the Great Dane. Where some breeds and types of dogs can get by on average foods, Great Danes and other rapidly growing breeds simply must have a good diet if they are to grow into their genetic potential, physically and mentally.

Without a good diet, Great Danes cannot attain their huge size and impressive musculature. It is also true that dogs that have been neglected nutritionally may also suffer in their

Feeding a Great Dane correctly involves special dietary considerations (such as monitoring protein levels for pups) throughout the life of the dog.

mental development as well. Since your dog will have to depend on you for what it eats, it is important that you understand what is needed by your Dane and why.

Special Feeding Considerations for Great Danes

While opinions vary among Great Dane breeders, there is some validity to the idea that feeding a young Great Dane (or any of several other fast-growing breeds) is much more difficult than feeding their more average-sized cousins. It seems that rapidly growing dogs, if fed a diet too high in protein, may put on muscle and tissue somewhat faster than their skeletal structures can grow to support the weight.

The problem that is faced in this situation is that the other extreme is just as bad. If you don't feed enough protein for the muscles and tissues to develop, then the Dane can remain spindly without the true physique of the "Apollo of Dogdom." Fortunately, a number of premium dog food companies now offer special foods for large-breed puppies. Several also have diets for large-breed adult dogs. Consult your veterinarian, your dog's breeder, or pet store.

CHECKLIST

Balance—The Key to Good Nutrition

Because our dogs are totally dependent on us for all the food they eat, we must be absolutely certain that the diets we use are balanced. Balanced dog foods are those that scientifically contain all the necessary protein, carbohydrates, fats, vitamins, and minerals your Great Dane will need first to grow up to giant proportions, then maintain an active and healthy metabolism. There are a few major rules to follow in determining a successful feeding plan for your Dane. To avoid a poor diet and to establish a nutritionally sound feeding regimen, adhere to these basic principles:

1 Feed your Great Dane a premium-quality, nutritionally balanced dog food.

2 As long as a particular food is meeting your dog's need, be consistent and stick with it. Don't constantly jump around from brand to brand.

3 Don't overfeed, and *avoid table scraps!*

The Elements of Good Canine Nutrition

There are several components or elements that make up a sound nutritional feeding program for your Great Dane. If any one of these elements is neglected or ignored, your dog's diet cannot be described as either sound or balanced. These elements are:

✔ Proteins (keeping in mind the special needs or constraints of a rapidly growing youngster).
✔ Carbohydrates.
✔ Fats.
✔ Vitamins and minerals.
✔ Water.
✔ Owner knowledge.
✔ Owner consistency.

Protein

Protein provides your Great Dane with the key amino acids that are so necessary for:
✔ its progression through the formative stages of its life.
✔ the continued sustaining of healthy bone and muscle.
✔ the body's own repair functions on bone and muscle.
✔ the production of infection-fighting antibodies.
✔ the production of needed hormones and enzymes that aid in natural chemical processes within the dog's body.

Carbohydrates

Carbohydrates provide fuel for your Great Dane's physical motor. Thoroughly cooked grain and vegetable products, as well as processed starches, provide the source for most of the carbohydrates in premium-quality pet foods.

When feeding your Dane, beware of overserving—foods with protein levels that are too high can be dangerous.

Along with fats, carbohydrates are the elements in your Dane's diet that give it usable energy. Carbohydrates are measured by caloric count or more simply, in calories.

Fats

The fats in your pet's diet provide a much more concentrated energy source than do carbohydrates. In fact, the same amount of fat will provide *twice* as much usable energy as a like amount of carbohydrates. The key vitamins A, D, E, and K are delivered by the fats in your Great Dane's meals. These are known as "fat soluble" vitamins and are useful in helping to develop and maintain a healthy skin and coat.

Fats are also of special importance in maintaining a dog's nervous system, but are equally significant in making dog foods more palatable. The dog foods that taste good are those more readily eaten by dogs, thus allowing a food to not only be nutritious and balanced but enjoyable. Finally, fat levels are often measured against the general activity level of a dog with the stresses of obedience work, breeding, and the show ring requiring more fats than those required for a stay-at-home "couch potato."

Vitamins and Minerals

While vitamins and minerals are certainly needed by your Great Dane for the general functioning of its body, vitamins are one of those good things that can be easily overdone. All the things a dog normally needs are supplied in a regular diet of a premium-quality

dog food. Unless your veterinarian indicates otherwise, *don't* add to the vitamin and mineral levels of a good food. Not only do additional supplementation generally not do any good, but they can actually do harm.

Water

Clean, fresh water is vitally important to the health of your Great Dane. Your dog will need lots of good water available to it at all times. Make pure and clean water as crucial a part of your pet's diet as any of the others. Keep water bowls full, disinfected, and close by for the good health of your Dane.

Owner Knowledge

Feeding a giant dog brings with it giant responsibilities. Not only do rapidly growing young Danes need different diets than their more average-sized counterparts, but your Great Dane's health throughout its life may largely depend on your knowledge of the food you feed it. Your Dane will be totally dependent on you for everything it regularly eats. Your awareness of its nutritional requirements

Just as training and care are crucial to producing an excellent Great Dane, so is feeding an essential factor.

TIP

Changing Dog Foods

While various experts disagree on the length of time you should take to make a dog food change, one good way is to do this over a month's time. Not only is a month easy to use because you have four weeks to serve as time lines to follow, but this roughly corresponds with the amount of time some professionals believe it takes to make a new food acceptable to dogs. The key word here is *gradual.* Go from an old diet to a new diet slowly and in increasingly larger percentages over an extended period of time.

---

and which foods can best meet those needs will be a key part—perhaps *the* key part—of your job for your pet.

Owner Consistency

Unfortunately for many dogs, their diet is comprised of whatever is on sale. While most dogs can survive on the constant switching of their foods, they will simply not thrive on such a practice. This is even truer for breeds like the Great Dane that have been so genetically altered from the norm. While all dogs, purebred and mixed breeds alike, deserve consistent feeding of a quality food, for a Great Dane this is of even greater importance. The physical structure of a giant dog needs a lot of consistent sustenance to first develop and then to continue functioning.

Commercial Dog Foods

There are hundreds of pet food products available. Some are high-quality, balanced foods that may be just what you and your Great Dane are seeking. Others are inferior products that are best avoided by a dog owner in search of a nutritionally complete diet for a special pet.

One of the pluses of using a premium-quality food is that these foods normally have a toll-free number that can connect you with people experienced in canine nutrition. Don't hesitate to use these numbers to ascertain what food to feed or to ask questions about a food your Dane is already being fed.

One of the greatest truths about dog food is the old axiom, "You get what you pay for!" This is certainly true about pet foods generally and about the premium level products you will want to feed your Great Dane. Don't spend a great

An elevated feeding bowl helps your Dane eat its food without ingesting too much air which could be a factor in bloat.

deal of time and money finding a Great Dane, adequately housing it, providing medical care, and so forth, and then take the cheap way out when it comes to the important concept of feeding your companion/pet. Generally, over the long run, the premium quality dog foods are actually a much better bargain than the sale products that may seem such a good deal.

Commercial dog foods generally come in two main forms: canned and dry. Each has some advantages and disadvantages.

Canned Dog Food

Canned dog food (sometimes called wet food) is the most palatable and the most expensive way to feed your Great Dane. Canned food generally smells really good to a dog and usually is eaten with gusto, but because of its high moisture rating of between 75 to 85 percent, it can also spoil quickly, even at room temperature. For a giant dog, a diet of exclusively canned food could be quite an expensive proposition. Additionally, the stool firmness and odor of canned food is usually the worst of any of the three forms of dog food.

Canned food is convenient and its long shelf life makes it easy to keep for long periods of time. Canned food diets also tend to contribute to more dental problems than does dry dog food. Most canned food is used as an additive or mixer with dry dog food for really large breeds of dogs.

Dry Dog Food

Dry dog food is the most cost-effective and most popular form of dog food, especially among large dog breeders. There are a good many dry foods on the market that can be truly described as complete dog diets with real nutritional balance. Dry foods also keep well without refrigeration, which isn't true for partially used canned foods. Dry foods have somewhat of a drawback in palatability, and dogs that have been fed only canned diets may have to be taught to eat dry foods.

Because dry dog foods require more use of a pet's teeth, this form contributes somewhat to better dental health and tartar reduction on a dog's teeth.

Note: Information from some dry dog food manufacturers notwithstanding, feeding dry food alone is not enough to keep your dog's teeth in good shape (see page 86).

Stool quality with premium-quality dry food is usually the best to be found in any form of dog diet. Digestibility is usually quite good, and puppies started on dry food readily eat it all their lives. Dry dog food does, however, have a moisture rating of only about 10 percent, making the need for good, fresh water for Great Danes all the more important.

Homemade Diets and Leftovers

Many dog breeders with years of experience will develop their own concoctions for their pets to eat. However, unless you are a trained canine nutritionist or you are a dog breeder with loads of experience and dog food knowledge, leave homemade diets alone. They are little more than nutritionally lacking meals of disguised table scraps.

Table scraps: Table scraps have absolutely no place in a balanced canine diet. Such ill-considered snacks can keep a dog from eating the right amount of its balanced food or even, in some cases, throw the regular diet's balance completely out of kilter. It is also true that feeding table scraps to your Great Dane may very well cause the big dog to expect to eat not only what you do, but when you do, and possibly where you do. Your dog should eat from its dish at the regular time that you set for it to eat.

Treats: Among treats that *can* be given safely and appropriately to your Great Dane are quality dog biscuits. Such biscuits are not only nutritionally good for your diet, but they are balanced to fit with the dog's regular diet. Follow the same rules with biscuits that you do with dog food; find a kind the dog will like and stay with them, and don't overdo it on the biscuits. Less is better than more.

Chews: Chews, such as the various nylon, rubber, and rawhide items, do not necessarily fall into the category of treats. They will, however, be good for your dog. Along with providing some benefit in tartar removal (not to replace regular dental care), these items also help a teething puppy or a bored adult find a suitable alternative to the furniture to chew on.

Feeding Great Dane Puppies (Under Two Years Old)

There are several good foods for large breed puppies available. Using these special diets should make feeding your young Dane much simpler and better than in earlier years. There are two key points to remember about feeding puppies:

1. When you bring your Dane pup home, by all means get some of the same food it was fed at the breeder's. Changing diets for a puppy is tantamount to changing baby formula with a human infant. You don't do it unless you absolutely have no choice! If you continue the puppy on the same food that it has been eating, you will reduce the transition shock that will already be in effect when your puppy leaves the only home it has ever known and moves with you to yours.

2. The second rule is similar to the first. Don't change your pup's food without an extremely good reason and then only with the intention of finding a puppy food that it will stay with until it reaches adulthood and goes on grown-up dog food. Responsible dog food sellers would prefer not to even give you a sample of their puppy food unless you are noticing a definite problem with what the puppy is eating now. The reason for this is both for your pup's benefit and for the benefit of the food seller. A radical, abrupt change in what a puppy is eating will almost always bring on some upset in the dog's digestive system usually expressed in the form of diarrhea.

Young puppies will need to be fed about four times a day with a quality food. As puppies grow older, the number of feedings can be reduced to three and then finally to two as they approach adulthood. There may be other formats for feeding certain strains or families of Danes. Your Dane mentor/friend can help you find a schedule that meets both your pup's needs and yours.

Feeding Adult Great Danes (Between Two and Five Years Old)

For some dogs adulthood comes more quickly than for others. Some people believe that a Great Dane will be near maturity at a little over one year. Because of the unique problems of skeletal growth being possibly exceeded by muscular growth, feeding still maturing youngsters according to the strict suggestions of experienced Dane people and canine nutrition experts is wise.

Normally, an adult dog will receive two feedings a day. If your Dane is a prime show dog being actively campaigned at different locations each weekend, its needs will be different from the spayed or neutered Dane that lives a less active (and stressful) pet existence. The metabolism of some dogs, even littermates, may be such that some dogs will need more food than others. You can gauge this only by living with and observing the food needs of your pet.

Feeding Older Danes (Five Years Old and Older)

An older Great Dane's metabolism may begin to slow as it ages. At this point in life, the dog will need more carbohydrates and less fat in its food. There are many quality dog foods designed for older canines. These should be useful for your Great Dane, if fed moderately and consistently.

As stated, spayed and neutered Danes will usually require a diet much like that of older dogs regardless of the pet's age. Remember, continued exercise is essential for neutered animals. Also remember in feeding older pets (and spays and neuters) that a fat Dane is not a healthy Dane. Added weight make the dog's internal organs have to work harder to do their jobs. A large, obese dog will also put more pressure on its feet and legs and joints and contribute to laming conditions.

As with any other diet problem, such as food allergies, your best ally will be your Dane's veterinarian. Long before your dog begins to have weight-related problems, discuss a possible feeding program with your dog's doctor. You may also want to avail yourself of the knowledge of experienced Dane people you know to discover how they handle feeding their aging dogs.

HEALTH CARE FOR YOUR GREAT DANE

Ironically, this giant among dogs will require very specific and highly consistent medical care throughout its life to remain in the best shape. Health care is just another reason that a careless or neglectful person should never own a Great Dane. Danes deserve owners that will proactively and continually seek out good veterinary care for the pet and then follow the advice of that practitioner.

Special Health Needs

As in other areas of Great Dane ownership, giant dogs bring giant responsibilities with regard to medical care. Not every person can even get an immobile or unconscious dog weighing well over 100 pounds (45 kg) *into* an automobile to take it to a veterinary clinic. Giant dogs, in a way not unlike very tiny dogs, need specialized preventive and treatment measures not usually necessary for dog breeds within the broad "average" category of size. A good preventive focus to hopefully stop health problems before they occur, a medical care "team" to deal with ongoing health issues or conditions unavoidable, and a specific medical

Your Great Dane's veterinarian will be a key element in avoiding illnesses and injuries and treating those problems that do arise.

plan are all needed to help ensure the Dane's well-being.

Keeping Your Great Dane Healthy

Your Great Dane deserves a safe and healthy existence. You and your family must learn accident prevention techniques and concepts. You will need to know about parasites, disease, and other medical conditions that may attack your pet.

The Veterinarian

Choosing a veterinarian for your Great Dane is a key decision. Most veterinary practitioners are skillful, caring professionals who offer sound care and treatment to their animal patients and solid information and guidance to their patient's owners. For your Great Dane, you will want just a little more. The health needs of giant dogs are somewhat different from the needs of many other dogs. If at all possible, try to find a veterinarian who not only has had experience with a number of the "giant" breeds (Danes, Irish Wolfhounds, Saint Bernards, Mastiffs, and so forth), but likes big dogs as well.

Diseases and Immunizations

Not only are inoculations against an array of dog-harming or dog-killing diseases a pivotal part of your Great Dane's preventive health plan, in most places some of these illness-fighting shots are the law!

Your Great Dane puppy should have its first immunizations at about six weeks of age while still at its first home—the breeder from whom you purchased it. These initial shots were beginning vaccinations for distemper, parvovirus, canine hepatitis, leptospirosis, parainfluenza, coronavirus, and bordetella.

Don't believe for a second that this initial round of inoculations completes your pup's immunization requirements. Preventing these diseases will necessitate follow-up shots (usually at eight to ten weeks and then again at twelve weeks). Another crucial immunization, that for rabies, usually takes place between three and six months. Annual boosters may be needed for some shots.

Your puppy's shot record should be a part of the permanent paperwork that you obtain when you get the puppy itself. The same thing is true if you should obtain an adult Great Dane. Your pet's veterinarian needs to know what vaccinations, or any other treatments,

your dog has received before you became its owner. This complete accounting of what has been done to and for your Great Dane will form the foundation of your pet's health records that should be kept current and accurate for the entire life of the dog.

The veterinarian will set up a schedule for these life-saving shots. Your diligence in seeing that your young Dane is on hand to get its immunizations will be the key to the good health of your puppy. If you forget or neglect this important task, you are putting your pet at great risk.

Distemper

Distemper has a long history of tragic consequences to the world of dogs. It was once the deadliest disease-enemy of puppies and young dogs. This extremely infectious and widely spread viral disease affects dogs and all other canines, as well as some other warm-blooded animals. Raging through kennels some decades back, distemper could kill a majority of the young dogs and all of the puppies. Once thus struck by distemper, some kennels never recovered and went out of existence along with the lives of most of their youngsters.

Veterinary medicine was able to develop an immunization that has greatly lowered the number of cases of this dread killer, but the inoculations work only if they are used. Distemper still occurs in places where dogs aren't adequately vaccinated or in wild animal populations.

A dog not immunized could begin to show symptoms as quickly as a week after coming into contact with an animal infected with distemper. Initially distemper might seem like just a cold with a runny nose and a little fever. In most cases, the dog would "go off its feed" or simply cease eating altogether. Listlessness and an appearance of fatigue would probably be observable, with diarrhea in evidence in some dogs.

Distemper was once called "hard pad disease" because of the thickening rigidity of the skin on the dog's nose and foot pads. Long known to dog breeders, distemper would sometimes throw a cruel twist into its pattern of infection. Occasionally a dog would seem to recover from the viral infection, start to regain strength, then slide back into nervous twitching, convulsions, paralysis, and finally death.

Veterinary science has done much to eliminate distemper from the lives of dogs and dog owners. Vaccination and yearly booster shots have made this killer of puppies and young dogs much less of a threat. Your Great Dane deserves a better fate than betting its life against distemper.

Rabies

Very few diseases evoke the level of fear that rabies, the dreaded "madness" of hydrophobia, can. Mental pictures of once-faithful dogs turning into mouth-foaming, raging monsters is still entrenched deep in the minds of people who remember when most pets were not inoculated against this acutely infectious, almost certainly fatal disease. Movies such as *Ol Yeller, Rage,* and *Cujo* have reinstilled the vivid imagery of rabies into the minds of people to whom rabies has mistakenly been considered a disease of the past.

Rabies is most often transmitted through the saliva of an infected animal, which passes the disease on by biting some other creature. Most warm-blooded mammals, including human beings, can be potential victims of rabies, but it is thought to be most often spread through skunks, bats, raccoons, foxes, unvaccinated cats and dogs, and other small animals.

In some places, rabies is still relatively widespread with outbreaks of the disease surfacing every few years. Other areas, such as England, have effectively eradicated rabies largely through a widespread prevention program and stern quarantine restrictions. Until 1885, when Louis Pasteur developed the first vaccine against rabies, this disease meant almost certain death. Before its fatal outcome rabies would present certain classic signs. The first of these was the symptom that gave the disease its technical name—hydrophobia, "a fear of water." Two phases also were usually seen: the *furious* phase when the animal would attack anything and everything around it. Sometimes the infected animal died in this phase, but if not, rabies progressed into the second phase— the *dumb* or more inactive stage which ends in paralysis, coma, and death.

Your Great Dane is a large and generally active dog. Rabies in such an animal would represent a significant threat to you, your family, and others. Immunization at three to six months, with another inoculation at the age of one year followed by annual rabies shots thereafter will protect your Dane from this horrible and now so unnecessary death.

Leptospirosis

This disease, which primarily damages the kidneys, is commonly spread through drinking or coming into contact with water contaminated by the urine of an infected animal. Symptoms of leptospirosis are: loss of appetite; fever; vomiting and diarrhea, and abdominal pain.

In advance cases, leptospirosis can quite severely damage the liver and kidneys, with resultant jaundice, weakened hind quarters, mouth sores and weight loss. Immunization for leptospirosis and annual booster shots are usually enough to protect your Great Dane.

Hepatitis (CAV-1)

Infectious canine hepatitis can affect any member of the canine family and can be contracted by dogs at any age. The severity of hepatitis, which is not the same illness of the same name that affects humans, can range from a relatively mild sickness to a quickly fatal viral infection that can take the life of an infected dog within 24 hours from onset of the illness.

Infectious canine hepatitis symptoms can include listlessness, fever, blood in stools and vomitus, abdominal pain, light sensitivity of the eyes, and tonsillitis. As an infectious disease, hepatitis can be spread by contact with the feces or urine of an infected animal.

Immunization with a yearly booster is a good preventive measure.

Parvovirus

This viral disease is a serious killer, especially of puppies, but it can mean death to an unvaccinated or untreated dog at any age. Parvovirus primarily attacks the gastrointestinal tract, but can also damage the heart. Puppies with parvovirus can suffer from severe dehydration from bloody, watery diarrhea and vomiting, and may die within 48 hours after the onset of the disease.

While good veterinary care can save some parvovirus victims, immunization is a much better course of action. If your unimmunized Great Dane puppy were to encounter a parvovirus-infected dog, a debilitating disease with potentially fatal consequences could result. Puppy vaccination followed by annual follow-up shots should keep parvovirus away from your pet.

Parainfluenza

Sometimes identified (incorrectly) under the name *kennel cough*, parainfluenza is a highly infectious viral disease that can rapidly rage through a dog population, as in a kennel or home where several dogs live. It is thought to be spread by contact with infected animals and the places they live as well as through the air. Parainfluenza causes a condition called tracheobronchitis, which is usually identified by a dry, hacking cough followed by retching as an

Responsible Great Dane ownership requires an awareness of potential health dangers that will confront your dog and making sure the dog gets the best possible medical care in a timely and consistent manner.

attempt to cough up throat mucus. In and of itself, parainfluenza is not usually a serious illness. Untreated, however, tracheobronchitis can weaken a dog and make it vulnerable to other ailments and infections.

Parainfluenza is preventable by vaccination in the puppy series with annual re-inoculation. Treatment for this disease is best supplied by a veterinarian with the patient isolated from other dogs to decrease the chances of further contagion.

Coronavirus

Unvaccinated dogs of any age can be affected by this contagious disease, which can cause severe diarrhea with watery, loose, foul-smelling, bloody stools. Coronavirus is sometimes mistaken for parvovirus and may leave a dog in such a weakened condition that parvovirus or other infections may occur.

Treatment by your Great Dane's veterinarian is usually successful, but immunization by vaccine is the preferred course. By preventing this relatively mild ailment, you may be able to avoid putting your pet at risk for some of the more serious medical problems.

Bordetella

Bordetella is a bacterial infection often observed in the presence of tracheobronchitis. Bordetella may make treatment of the parainfluenza-induced tracheobronchitis more difficult. Protect your Dane from this infectious "fellow traveler" by availing your pet of the immunization that does much to prevent its occurrence.

Lyme Disease

Lyme disease is a serious, potentially fatal disease that affects warm-blooded animals and humans. Since your Great Dane can often greatly benefit from a walk in the park or any wooded area, the possibility of exposure to Lyme disease must be considered. This ailment could even be contracted in your pet's own backyard.

Lyme disease was first identified in Lyme County, Connecticut, and is spread by the deer tick, a tiny little bloodsucker credited with carrying an illness that can do your Dane, or even you, great physical harm! Spirochetosis, the technical name for this disease, can affect your dog in several ways, but usually a swelling and tenderness around the joints is observable. If you find a tick on your dog that has not been Lyme-immunized, or suspect that the dog has been bitten by a tick, immediate veterinary care is advisable.

If you have been bitten by a tick, or evidence the telltale tick bite with its characteristic surrounding of red (somewhat like a bull's eye on a target), take the same action, substituting your physician or county health department for the veterinarian. In both cases, yours and the dog's, timely diagnosis and treatment is essential.

Other Medical Conditions, Illnesses, and Health Concerns

Bloat/Gastric Tortion

Bloat or gastric tortion is a very serious health concern for all of the large, deep-chested breeds of dogs, which includes the Great Dane. Bloat, which has been known to painfully kill an otherwise healthy dog in just a few hours, involves a swelling of the dog's stomach from gas or water or both. Bloat remains somewhat of a mystery apparently brought on by a wide variety of suggested causes that may work independently of one another or in combination. Some of these are

✔ A large intake of food followed by a large intake of water followed by strenuous exercise.

✔ A genetic predisposition in some breeds and even within some families within some breeds.

✔ Stress, brought about by many things (one English Great Dane authority even suggested that thunder could be a contributing factor to bloat).

✔ The sex and age of the dog seems to be a factor as males seem to be affected more than females and dogs over 24 months more susceptible than younger animals.

Regardless of the causes, bloat remains a real killer of large-breed dogs. Some bloat symptoms are

✔ Obvious abdominal pain and noticeable abdominal swelling.

✔ Excessive salivation and rapid breathing.

✔ Pale and cool-to-the-touch skin in the mouth.

✔ A dazed and "shocky" look.

A dog with bloat needs immediate care if it is to stand any chance of survival. Transport your Dane *immediately* to the nearest veterinarian!

Hip Dysplasia

Hip dysplasia, or HD, is another major canine health problem. While it does not have the usually fatal consequences of gastric tortion, HD can be quite painful and debilitating. HD is a medical condition in which the hip joint is slack or loose, combined with a deformity of the socket of the hip and the femoral head joining the thighbone. Malformed development of the hip's connecting tissues leaves an unstable hip joint. Instead of being a stable receptacle, fitting like a cup for the end of the thighbone, the HD-affected hip socket is usually quite shallow. HD can cause a wobbling, unsteady gait that can be very painful to the dog.

HD is thought to be clearly inherited, but it must be acknowledged that not every puppy produced by dysplastic parents will have HD itself. It is also true that some nondysplastic parents will produce some dysplastic puppies.

HD cannot always be discovered until a puppy is two years old. The Orthopedic Foundations for Animals (OFA) has developed a widely used X-ray method of determining the presence or absence of HD. You should get a Great Dane puppy from a mating in which both parents have been tested and found free of this condition. This should reduce the chances of your pup having this painful malady.

Diarrhea and Vomiting

Some diarrhea and vomiting is the result of ordinary things such as changes in food or some added stress. In puppies, vomiting and diarrhea can also be commonly caused by internal parasites. Even so, both diarrhea and vomiting can be early warning signals of more serious ailments.

Any extended period (more than 12 to 24 hours) of vomiting or diarrhea should alert you to the need for a quick trip to the veterinarian. Even if this early alarm is a false one, the next one may not be.

Anal Sac Impaction

The anal glands lie just under the skin on each side of the anus. Normally these sacs are emptied naturally when the dog defecates. When these sacs become stopped up or impacted, they must be emptied by hand of their strong-smelling secretions. One sign of impacted anal sacs is when a dog scoots along the floor dragging its rear end. The anal sacs can be emptied by your veterinarian or you could easily learn to do this yourself.

Inherited Conditions

Almost every breed of dog will have one or more conditions that are passed along genetically from generation to generation. A tendency toward bloat or hip dysplasia could be examples of just such inherited conditions. You need to be all the more certain when purchasing a young Great Dane that it comes from parents that have no apparent physiological deformities or other factors that could become a negative inheritance for their offspring.

Internal Parasites

Dogs and puppies often have worms. Worms are parasites that draw their sustenance off your pet and they can lead to some serious health problems. Through some simple tests, your veterinarian cannot only detect the presence of worms, but can also prescribe an appropriate treatment that will lead to their elimination.

Note: Let your veterinarian treat your Great Dane for worms. Even though various worm treatments are available on the market, your dog's doctor will best know how to treat your pet for these parasites in the most effective and safest manner.

Regular checkups will spot most parasites, but if you suspect that your Great Dane is being bothered by a parasitic infestation, don't wait until the next regular visit. The sooner your veterinarian confirms your suspicions and starts treatment, the better for your dog.

Worms are usually discovered by examination of your dog's stools or blood. The most common worms affecting dogs are: roundworms, hookworms, tapeworms, and heartworms. Each of these parasites must be dealt with in its own specific way, which is best identified and handled by your veterinarian.

Roundworms

Even though dogs of all ages can have a roundworm infestation, puppies are the most common target of roundworms. Puppies often get roundworms even before they are born, since an infected mother dog can pass these parasites along to her offspring prenatally.

Roundworms are like weights pulling down a puppy's vitality, as pups with roundworms simply will not thrive. Roundworms may take away the sharp and shiny look that a healthy puppy should have. A pendulous abdomen or potbelly may look cute on a puppy, but it is also a possible indication of roundworms. Puppies with roundworms may pass some of them through their stools or when they vomit. Recognize that roundworms sap the vim and vigor, and possibly the overall health, of your Dane puppy who needs every edge it can get to grow up into a good representative of a giant breed. If you discover roundworms, don't delay—get your puppy into a veterinarian's care to rid it of the health-robbing interlopers.

Another thing you can do to prevent roundworm infestation is to practice good kennel hygiene. Keep the puppy's area extremely clean and sanitary. Be especially vigilant in quickly and appropriately disposing of any and all stools.

Hookworms

Another uninvited internal pest that can strike at dogs of any age, but really hurts puppies is the hookworm. Puppies with hookworms will have bloody or tarlike stools and will also fail to thrive. Hookworm-infested puppies don't eat properly and fail to keep their weight.

Since hookworms are actually tiny vampires that attach themselves to the insides of the small intestines and literary suck blood, they can rapidly reduce a puppy to a greatly weakened state. Anemia is a sometimes fatal consequence of leaving hookworms untreated in a puppy.

Your veterinarian knows how to handle these little bloodsuckers and how to put your puppy on the road to a healthy adulthood. As with hookworms, cleanliness is a definite part of a successful treatment plan, so get rid of stools as soon as possible.

Tapeworms

Fleas are the common host for tapeworms and can share these parasites with your dog. Though they rarely severely debilitate a dog, these flat, segmented parasites steal from your dog's health. A dog with tapeworms cannot be at its best. If you care for and want to see your Great Dane grow to its full potential, then tapeworms are your adversary in this goal. Eliminating tapeworms from your dog will give it the added vitality to remain healthy.

Consult your veterinarian about a treatment plan for the elimination of tapeworms. Also ask about how to do away with the parasite that brought its own parasite to your pet—the flea. The elimination of a recurrent tapeworm infestation is just another good reason for also eliminating fleas from your dog's life.

Heartworms

Another parasite of a parasite, the heartworm comes to your pet from its original host, the mosquito. A heartworm-infested mosquito bites your dog and passes along the heartworm larvae into your pet's bloodstream and ultimately to the bloodstream's pump—the heart.

Because you will probably not want to keep your Great Dane in a mosquito-free inside environment for all of its life, a mosquito with heartworm larvae is ready to share its ever-present threat in an ever-expanding area of this country. The odds are greatly against your pet's being outside in an area where heartworms exist and not contracting these worms. Left untreated heartworms will almost literally strangle your dog's heart and certainly cause its premature death.

Your veterinarian can help you with a plan that will prevent heartworm infestation. This involves your regular administering of medicine to kill heartworms. It must be given to a dog that does not yet have an infestation and could do an already affected dog great harm.

Treatment for heartworms is a long, potentially risky, and sometimes expensive procedure. Prevention is, by far, the better course of action and could save your Great Dane from an early and miserable death.

External Parasites

Fleas

Fleas are the bane of many a dog's life. They are the most common external parasite afflicting dogs and they actually feed on your Great Dane's blood. In extreme cases, fleas can bring about anemia in your dog and in almost all

Many breed authorities, veterinarians, and animal nutritionists recommend that young Danes be fed low protein diets to avoid developing too much muscle mass for their still growing skeletal frames.

cases do make a dog's life miserable. Fleas add insult to their injury in that not only are they an external parasite, but they harbor and introduce the internal parasite—the tapeworm—into your dog. Some dogs (like some humans) can even have an extreme allergic reaction to flea bites.

Flea bite allergy makes its victim suffer far more than in the way fleas pester a nonallergic dog. This allergy can cause hair loss, skin problems, and incessant scratching. Immediate attention by a veterinarian is required to alleviate this extremely uncomfortable condition.

Dealing with fleas involves a "take charge and take no prisoners" mentality. The sooner you realize that it is an all-out war between you and the fleas, the sooner you can begin to attack these little parasites in every place in which they live. If your dog has fleas, everywhere that the dog goes will have fleas—its bed, the yard, the kennel, the car, and your home.

Failure to hit your flea enemy in any one of these battlefields—and probably several others that you can name—is as good as a complete failure. If fleas can survive in the yard, merely getting them out of the house is only a temporary victory. The fleas will be back in your house in no time.

By consulting with your veterinarian and perhaps someone in the pet supply business you should be able to obtain a variety of weapons in your flea war. Flea dips, flea shampoos, flea powder, flea collars, flea sprays are

all on-dog remedies. Their use should be coordinated by a call to your veterinarian and be based on the knowledge that fleas spend 90 percent of their time *off* your dog and 10 percent of their time *on* the dog.

To take care of the 90 percent of the time that fleas inhabit your yard, your car, your couch and so forth, you must use other products. Consult with your exterminator about how to handle fleas off the dog. Always use flea killers with great care and follow their directions implicitly!

Ticks

Ticks are another external parasite that can make a dog's life more uncomfortable. Like fleas, ticks also live on the host creature's blood. Because ticks are much larger than fleas, they suck more blood and can actually increase their size several hundred percent—all at the expense of your dog.

While ticks are generally just a nuisance, they can carry life-threatening disease (see Lyme Disease, page 77). They can also cause infectious sores and scars on your Dane if the ticks are removed incorrectly. Not only are these sores painful, but because of the Great Dane's short coat, they can also be somewhat unsightly.

Ticks can be prevented or eliminated fairly easily with the regular use of veterinarian-recommended on-dog sprays or dips, and living area treatments. It is important to remember never to simply pull a tick off your Dane. Doing so will probably leave part of the tick's mouth in your dog's skin which can lead to infection. To remove ticks follow these steps:

✔ Place a small amount of rubbing alcohol at the exact site of the tick bite. Be careful that the dog doesn't get any of this denatured alcohol into its mouth or eyes!

✔ After making certain that the pet will remain still, use tweezers to grab the tick as close to the dog's skin as possible, pulling *very* slowly on the tick's head and mouth.

✔ Be certain to get all of the tick out of your Dane's skin and then put additional alcohol or another antiseptic on the bite.

✔ Dispose of the tick in such a way that it will not get back on your dog or onto you!

✔ Sometimes you will see TWO ticks at one bite site—a large blood-engorged one (the female) and a small, often dark brown one (the male). Be sure to get all of both ticks out of your Dane's skin.

Ticks like to get into a Dane's large, and evidently tick-inviting ears. Always check your dog over carefully after any trips to the woods or to a park where ticks might be, or even after the dog has been in an untreated backyard.

Ear Mites

The prominent ears (trimmed or untrimmed) of your Great Dane can also be targets of another bothersome pest, the ear mite. These microscopic mites live in both the ear and the ear canal. Their presence can cause a dark, dirty-looking, waxy material to adhere to the inner skin of the ears. These ear mites can cause dogs a great deal of discomfort, as evidenced by excessive ear scratching and violent head-shaking in an attempt to shake loose these itchy little parasites.

Your Dane's veterinarian is your best line of defense against this rather easily treated parasitic invader. Regularly inspect your dog's ears and then seek professional help if these mites, which are usually transferred from contact with other animals, are present.

Mange

There are two common types of mange, both caused by another form of mite:

1. Red, or demodectic, mange—especially affects physically vulnerable pets, like young puppies or oldsters, with ragged, ugly-looking hair loss accompanied by sometimes severe itching.

2. Sarcoptic mange (also known as "scabies"—comes from a mite that actually burrows into the dog's outer layers of skin. Like red mange, scabies can cause a great deal of itching and hair loss. An additional negative to this kind of mange is that the highly contagious scabies mite doesn't confine itself just to pets; it can also be transmitted to pet owners!

Both these manges not only make your Dane uncomfortable and unsightly; they make the dog unhealthy. For example, if left untreated severe demodectic mange can become a systemic disease that could prove fatal. Seek the competent care of a veterinarian if your Great Dane seems to have mange and do so *immediately!*

Skin Problems

Great Danes are sometimes prone to develop other skin problems. These might be fungal in nature. Flea bite allergy or another allergy of some sort might cause a skin condition. Stress or some other environmental factor could even bring on a skin problem. Even the color of your Dane may be a partial cause for these situations. Blue dogs, in other breeds as well as in Danes, sometimes have more skin problems than their fawn or brindle peers.

Sometimes even what a dog eats could cause rashes or "hot spots" because some dogs definitely seem allergic to some food items.

You can avoid some skin problems by wisely choosing where you will buy your Great Dane. Good housekeeping and regular attention to your pet's coat can help spot problems and parasites before they get a good start. Conferring with your veterinarian, not only for after-the-fact treatment, but ahead of time will make skin problems less likely.

Emergency Care for Your Dane

The Team Approach

As mentioned earlier when discussing preventive care for your Dane, you will also need an emergency team to help you if an injury or immobilizing sickness befalls your pet.

Because of the sheer size of a Great Dane, you may want to line up some help from some of your sturdier neighbors. In some small towns you may be able to get someone from the police, fire, or sheriff's department to come out and give you a hand in getting a giant dog to medical care.

One Dane owner, not the largest of physical specimens herself, got several strapping lads from the local high school football team to help her. Another used an emergency-type gurney where he simply slid an older, almost comatose Dane onto a blanket and then onto the gurney, which transported the oldster to the owner's station wagon and on to the waiting veterinarian.

Some veterinarians may make house calls but in an emergency this may not be a possible alternative. Always ask your veterinarian what to do in transporting a sick or injured dog. Because they deal with such issues all the time, they may have options and alternatives you might not realize.

Giant Dogs Require More Emergency Planning

Everything about giant dog ownership seems to come in large pieces. One Dane owner found that she had to sell her treasured old Volkswagen and obtain a newer, larger car so that she could travel with her pet when the need arose. Because this owner always used the dog's carrier when it went places with her, and because there was no way to get this carrier into a VW, the change in vehicles became necessary.

Being prepared for the things that can happen to bigger dogs over their smaller cousins is not unlike the things that can happen to toddlers instead of infants. Bigger children can get into more potentially hurtful situations. The same thing is true for bigger dogs. After you have chosen a Dane-aware veterinarian, ask

this professional to help you with a first aid kit to handle the basic bumps and scratches that fall within the skill level of a pet's owner rather than necessitating a trip to the animal hospital.

Accidents

In even the best of dog-owner relationships, where much preventive care and dog-proofing has taken place, accidents will happen. When they do, you must be prepared.

The first rule in dealing with an injured canine: *Don't make things worse.* Rough handling can turn a simple fracture into a compound fracture, an injured back into paralysis, or a careless owner into an accident victim himself. As you assess the injury to your pet, try to do so with a clear head. This dog may mean the world to you, but if you really want

The mantled Great Dane (formerly called the "Boston") is also a derivative from harlequin breeding. Unlike the blue merle, the mantle now has complete acceptance in the show ring.

to help your pet, you must act rationally. Some of the smart moves to make around an injured pet are as follows:

✔ Speak in a calm and reassuring voice as your hurt and frightened dog will pick up on any hysteria that your voice or demeanor could convey.

✔ Always approach any injured animal slowly and deliberately, even if the pet and you have been friends for years. Speed may be important, but a dog bite can slow down the emergency-aid process appreciably.

✔ Gently, but securely muzzle the dog; a Dane-sized muzzle might be a good item for the first aid kit. If a regular muzzle isn't available, use a necktie, a belt, or something similar.

✔ Attend to any immediate bleeding (see Bleeding, page 85) in an appropriate fashion.

✔ If you have sufficient muscle power available, put the dog on a makeshift stretcher (a tabletop, a sturdy piece of plywood, or even a strong tarpaulin might work), securing the dog so it won't fall off.

✔ If you don't have any physical help, you'll have to figure out a way to transport an injured pet to your vehicle. Some experts suggest tenderly getting the dog onto a blanket or tarp and then sliding, pulling, or otherwise moving the pet as gently as possible to your car.

✔ Call your veterinarian to alert him or her that you are on your way and will need help getting into the clinic.

✔ Drive *safely* to the clinic. Don't aggravate your Dane's injuries or endanger yourself by race car driving.

Note: The source of most of the serious injuries to pets, even huge Great Danes, comes when these canines collide with another species—the automobile. By not allowing your dog to run free and by being especially alert in situations where your dog could run out into a busy street or highway, you can probably avoid this most deadly of interactions.

In areas where Great Danes live in or near rural areas, it becomes equally important to prevent accidents by keeping the Dane at home. A large fawn Great Dane looks astonishingly like a deer and during hunting season such a dog could be killed by a hunter in a case of mistaken identity.

Heatstroke

Your Great Dane pet can be your deceased ex-pet in a matter of only a few minutes if left inside an automobile with poor ventilation and high inside temperatures. This can happen in a short time on any sunny day, even when the whether is only moderately warm at 60°F (15.6°C). Even if the car windows are partially down, a dog can die from heatstroke in such an oven-hot situation. *Never* put your dog in such a uselessly dangerous and potential fatal situation!

Heatstroke symptoms include a dazed look and rapid, shallow panting with a high fever. The dog's gums will appear bright red.

Speed is now of the essence. You must act *immediately,* even before going to the nearest veterinarian. Lower the dog's temperature by pouring cool water or a mixture of cool water and alcohol over it, before heading to the animal hospital.

Bleeding

If your Great Dane appears to be bleeding, identify the source of the blood and apply firm but gently pressure to the area. Continued bleeding, any significant blood loss, or a gaping wound will require veterinary attention; treat any bleeding as a serious situation worthy of immediate action.

Poisoning

Your Great Dane is at risk in a number of ways, but never more so than in its own home and yard from accidental poisoning. Because we live in a chemical-laden society, there are any number of toxic materials that your pet could accidentally ingest that could do it great harm. The most ironic part of the poisoning danger is that some of the things that we normally have around the house, use every day, or even that we eat can kill a dog. Following are some of the most common toxic agents around the average dog's home:

✔ Antifreeze. It is extremely dangerous because it can leak out of the family car perhaps even without our knowledge. It is deadly poison to pets and has a taste than many dogs love.

✔ Chocolate. In sufficient amounts, it can kill even a giant dog like your Great Dane.

✔ A number of outside plants. These are dangerous, especially to a young Dane still in the chewing stages. Such landscaping standards such as azalea, rhododendron, holly, and other yard plants, can bring death to your pet if ingested. Even wild plants, such as mistletoe and poison ivy, have been known to bring out severe reactions in dogs. Check with your local county extension service for an up-to-date and area-relevant listing of potentially deadly plants that are either widely planted or that grow wild in your geographical area.

✔ Some houseplants. These can also be killers. Popular flowers and plants such as dieffen-bachia, poinsettia, and jade plants can be toxic. Before you bring a new pet into an area in which there are houseplants, check with a florist or nursery to be certain they will be safely compatible.

✔ Some household cleaners can also kill an inquisitive pet. Keep all solvents, insecticides, pesticides, and cleaners away from places where your Great Dane can go.

If your dog begins to act listless, has convulsions, or suffers from disoriented behavior, it may have been poisoned. Other symptoms include diarrhea, vomiting, and a change in color of the mucous membranes. If you see these signs hurry your pet to the veterinarian.

The Life Span of the Great Dane

Giant dogs do not have correspondingly long life spans. Sadly, a Great Dane is often an old dog when members of toy or other smaller breeds are just entering middle age. That your Dane, on average, may not live much past eight years old is a reality that you and your family must face when you decide to make a Great Dane a member of your family. Some Danes live longer than this, while others have even shorter natural lives.

All giant breeds seem to suffer from this decrease in life span while other large, but not giant dogs do not. Irish Setters, not a small breed by any description, seem to live much longer than do Great Danes. You can help yourself in this area by attempting to choose a Great Dane from a line or pedigreed family that tends to beat the age odds.

Old Age

When the inquisitive youngster of all legs and ears becomes the distinguished old, gray-muzzled veteran, your treatment of your pet Dane must be different. The old Dane will sleep a little more; play will be a little less vigorous. The oldster will still love its family and want to be included; it just can't go as fast as before.

A whole new set of issues will be important now: Your Dane may need a dog food for senior canines; its teeth and gums will need extra care; there may be some hearing loss and possible eye problems. Most of these can be handled by timely visits to the veterinarian and by your ongoing attention to the changing needs of your pet.

Areas Needing Your Ongoing Attention

Teeth

Your Great Dane will need good dental care all of its life. Tartar accumulation can bring on gum and tooth disease. You can lessen tartar and also greatly ensure good dental health for your dog by:

✔ Regularly inspecting your Great Dane's teeth and gums, not only for tartar, but for signs of tooth decay, foreign objects (usually pieces of wood from the dog's chewing on sticks and so forth).

✔ Cleaning your Great Dane's teeth at home.

✔ Regular veterinary dental checkups with occasional professional teeth cleaning to improve upon your efforts.

✔ The use of veterinarian-approved chew toys and dental exercisers, designed to help remove tartar and plaque.

✔ Feeding a good brand of dry dog food and dog biscuits that will use the dog's regular chewing and grinding action to help reduce tartar.

Eyes

The large, prominent eyes of the Great Dane will need some attention from you as the dog ages. Other than the puppy-proofing and Dane-proofing that should be a part of your regular regimen, you need to protect your dog from sharp objects that might be just at eye level. You also need to keep the Dane safe from toxic substances or fumes that can irritate or damage eyes.

Neighborhood children throwing stones or shooting an air rifle at what is probably the biggest dog in the neighborhood could do your Dane damage. Air pollution, thorny plants, heavy underbrush all have eye-damaging potential. Even aging itself could bring on problems such as cataracts. All of these eye problems can be greatly lessened in severity by regular eye inspections done by you and by your veterinarian during general checkups.

You may notice some mucus collecting in the corners of your Great Dane's eyes from time to time. This is usually a perfectly normal condition that can be simply dealt with by gentle wiping with a soft cloth. Don't, however, confuse this ordinary mucus-like material with an eye discharge that can signal an eye problem and that needs professional attention.

Ears

The ears of a Great Dane are among its most striking features. Whether your Dane has had its ears cropped like that of many show dogs, or whether your dog has its ears in their natural state, these ears will need regular attention and ongoing care from you. Dog ears are among the favorite hiding places of such parasites as ticks and ear mites (See Ticks, page 81, and Ear Mites, page 82). Regular inspection of the ears will let you spot these little invaders early and begin a plan to get rid of them.

Sometimes a male dog's ears will be a record of the hostile interactions it may have had with other male dogs. Also, because of their location—high up on either side of the dog's head—ears suffer some damage when a big, fast dog runs through underbrush. Always keep a close watch on your pet's ears for cuts or scratches that may need medical attention—yours or the veterinarian's.

Feet and Nails

Giant dogs bring giant responsibilities. While the feet of every dog will be better if the dog's owner gives them regular care, the feet of a huge dog that must often support weights of over 150 pounds (68 kg) *must* have good owner care. One owner of a large brindle male that weighed 187 pounds (85 kg) asserted, "If you don't think that the feet of a Great Dane take a lot of punishment, let my dog step on your foot with just one of his."

While a small dog might be able to get around on a bad foot or on a foot with an injured toenail, giant dogs have considerably more trouble when their running gear is not in good condition. Beginning with good nail care, which should start when the Great Dane is a puppy, down to preventive maintenance that keeps broken glass and other foot-harming items out of the dog's path, the care of a

Dane's feet is as important as any other part of its health plan.

Great Danes put a lot of stress on their footpads and on their nails. Regular inspections will let you know if your dog has suffered a slight abrasion that could later become a bigger foot problem. Regular nail trimming, which isn't difficult when the dog has had it done all its life, is a *must* for good foot care. You will need a Dane-worthy set of toenail clippers (either the scissors type or the "guillotine" type) and they should be used regularly as the dog's nails start to grow too long. Remember in nail trimming to keep well away from the "quick" of the main blood supply of the nail. You may have to use an emery board or nail file to shorten nails when the "quick" is too close for easy trimming.

Another aspect of foot care is to carefully look at your Dane's feet after a walk along a street or at a paved highway rest area. Sometimes, toxic substances, motor oil or antifreeze

Injuries and illnesses in giant dogs tend to be somewhat more difficult to handle because of the size of the patient.

can be picked up on a dog's feet. Then, if the dog licks off the offending substance, feet problems can become a possible poisoning.

Giving Your Dane Medicine

You should know how to give your Great Dane the medicines prescribed by its veterinarian for treatment or prevention purposes. Some dogs simply don't like to take medicine and will actually spit out pills and capsules. Some experienced dog medicine givers hide the pill or capsule in a dog treat such as bread covered with some canned dog food, or perhaps a little clump of semimoist food with the medicine hidden inside.

Other dog people take the more direct approach of opening the dog's mouth, slightly leaning its head back a short way, and then placing the pill as far back on the dog's tongue as they can reach. This accomplished, they then simply close the dog's mouth, speaking calmly, and wait for the dog to swallow.

Note: *Never* tilt the Dane's head far back and simply toss in the pill or capsule; this could cause the pill to go into the windpipe instead of down the throat.

Always faithfully follow the veterinarian's dosages and instructions carefully. Never use outdated medicines or give your Great Dane medication designed for humans or other animals without advance approval from your dog's veterinarian.

Saying Good-bye

That gangling puppy you chose will grow to become a majestic Great Dane and a full member of your family. Just as certainly, barring premature death from illness or accident, this

The life of your Great Dane is completely in your hands from puppyhood through an often all too quick adulthood into the dog's senior years. Each age phase will bring special joys and special responsibilities that a responsible and caring pet owner must recognize and handle.

majestic friend will grow to be an old Dane. In the best of all practical worlds every good old dog would live a full, healthy life and die painlessly in its sleep one night. In the real world, things don't always work out as we would hope.

Great Danes have been given much. Their beauty and regal strength is admired the world over. When the Dane grows old, its size sometimes tends to work against it. That great height and weight can become a burden for an old dog. For some Danes, the ravages of old age bring pain and discomfort to their last years.

Hopefully, your Great Dane will live out the best possible ending and never know a painful day in its life. If this does not occur and your old friend begins to suffer, a difficult choice has to be made. When living becomes unbearable for your pet, take your veterinarian's counsel and give serious consideration to ending the dog's suffering. Such a decision is never easy, but for the good of the dog a gentle, painless, humane end is far better than endless and acute discomfort.

Prevention of any medical problem is always better than an after-the-fact treatment approach. Because Great Danes are huge dogs, they can have huge problems. Preventing health problems for such a giant breed deals with several diverse aspects of Dane ownership:

1. Choosing a Dane from physically and temperamentally sound stock is an essential element in an effort to avoid some painful, expensive and heart-rending circumstances later. While no dog can be absolutely guaranteed to never develop serious medical problems throughout all of its life, choosing a puppy or an adult Great Dane with a poor medical heritage can greatly increase the likelihood of a negative health future.

2. Failing to adequately prepare for a rapid developing canine of a giant breed increases the possibility that accidents will happen and from these accidents dire consequences can result. For example, assuming that your Dane will always be a model canine citizen and never get into trouble when running free in a neighborhood is ludicrous. If you don't have your dog under some form of control or restraint at *all* outside times (a fence, a leash, combined with good training) medical problems are *certain* to come your dog's way and perhaps be fatal.

3. Regular medical care by a licensed veterinary practitioner will not only eliminate many negative medical conditions, but will also spot other situations that can become physical problems and devise treatment modalities with which these can be handled. No dog should go without immunizations and regular checkups.

4. Because of the demand placed on the metabolism, bones, and muscle tissue of a rapidly growing Great Dane, owners must become well-versed in dog nutrition generally and in Dane nutrition specifically. Failure to do so can, at the very least, produce an adult that doesn't quite meet the definition physically, mentally, or temperament-wise of what a Great Dane should be. In a worst case view, a poorly fed Dane puppy could grow into a pain-racked, stunted cripple that

Failure to clean up after a pet during walks or visits to the park is not only extremely bad manners, but also illegal in most places.

should probably be mercifully and humanely euthanized.

5. Failure to train a Great Dane, at least in basic commands for human control, is another aspect of creating a circumstance that can only have a negative health outcome for the Dane. A giant dog that doesn't obey can become a giant problem possibly with giant medical or legal repercussions.

6. Hoping for the best while preparing for the worst is a sound philosophy for a novice Dane owner. Even with the best of care, feeding, medical attention, training, and a safety-oriented environment a puppy or an adult dog can sometimes become injured or sick. While having a good working relationship with a Dane-aware veterinarian is part of an emergency plan, there are other factors that must be considered:

✔ Unless you are as large a human as your Dane is a dog, you may need help getting your sick or injured pet to the veterinary office. Not everyone will be willing or able to provide this help on the spur of the moment. Plan for just such circumstances, hoping that they will never occur.

✔ Knowledge of possible Dane-threatening conditions, such as gastric tortion (or bloat), is a mandatory precondition before becoming the owner of a Great Dane. Knowing about these

A simple fanny pack stocked with a few items is a great tool for preventive care. If you or your Dane become ill or injured while out on a walk, extra collars, IDs, and other items can literally be lifesavers.

things, certain preventives, and what to do if such problems arise must be part of any prevention plan.

✔ Making your home as accident-proof as possible for your Dane is an obvious aspect sometimes overlooked by potential (or even current) Dane owners. A large dog weighing as much or more than its owner with the potential to put its forepaws higher than an average person's head can get into potentially harmful predicaments. Size awareness plus general common sense methods of keeping pets out of trouble is crucial information for a would-be Dane owner.

INFORMATION

Organizations

International Kennel Clubs
Great Dane Club of America*
Marie A. Fint
442 Country View Lane
Garland, Texas 75043
   *This address may change with the election of new club officers. The current listing can be obtained by contacting the American Kennel Club.

American Kennel Club
5580 Centerview Drive
Suite 200
Raleigh, North Carolina 27606
Phone: (919) 233-9767
Fax: (919) 233-3740
E-mail: info@akc.org
Web site: *www.akc.org*

Australian Kennel Club
Royal Show Ground
Ascot Vale
Victoria, Australia

Canadian Kennel Club
89 Skyway Avenue
Suite 100
Etobicoke, Ontario M9W 6R4
Canada
Phone: (416) 675-6506

The Kennel Club (England)
1-4 Clarges Street
Picadilly
London, W7Y 8AB
England

New Zealand Kennel Club
P.O. Box 523
Wellington, 1
New Zealand

Information and Printed Material
American Boarding Kennel Association
4575 Galley Road, Suite 400 A
Colorado Springs, Colorado 80915
(Publishes lists of approved boarding kennels.)

American Society for the Prevention of Cruelty
   to Animals (ASPCA)
424 East 92nd Street
New York, New York 10128
(212) 876-7700

American Veterinary Medical Association
1931 North Meacham Road, Suite 100
Schaumberg, Illinois 60173
(847) 925-8070

Gaines TWT
P.O. Box 8172
Kankakee, Illinois 60901
   (Publishes *Touring with Towser,* a directory of hotels and motels that accommodate guests with dogs.

Humane Society of the Unites States (HSUS)
2100 L Street NW
Washington, DC 20037

Books

In addition to the most recent edition of the official publication of the American Kennel Club, *The Complete Dog Book,* published by Howell House, Inc., New York, other suggestions include

Alderton, David. *The Dog Care Manual.* Hauppauge, New York: Barron's Educational Series, Inc., 1986.

Baer, Ted. *Communicating with Your Dog.* Hauppauge, New York: Barron's Educational Series, Inc., 1989.

___. *How to Teach Your Old Dog New Tricks.* Hauppauge, New York: Barron's Educational Series, Inc., 1991.

Frye, Fredric. *First Aid for Your Dog.* Hauppauge, New York: Barron's Educational Series, Inc., 1987.

Klever, Ulrich. *The Complete Book of Dog Care.* Hauppauge, New York: Barron's Educational Series, Inc., 1989.

___. *Dogs: A Mini Fact Finder.* Hauppauge, New York: Barron's Educational Series, Inc., 1990.

Pinney, Chris C. *Guide to Home Pet Grooming.* Hauppauge, New York: Barron's Educational Series, Inc., 1990.

Ullmann, Hans. *The New Dog Handbook.* Hauppauge, New York: Barron's Educational Series, Inc., 1984.

Wrede, Barbara, *Civilizing Your Puppy.* Hauppauge, New York: Barron's Educational Series, Inc., 1992.

Other Great Dane Reading

Hart, Ernest H. *This Is The Great Dane.* Jersey City, New Jersey: TFH Publications, Inc., 1967.

Lanning, Jean. *Great Danes.* London: John Gifford Ltd., 1974.

Basquette, Lina. *Your Great Dane.* Fairfax, Virginia: Denlinger's, 1972.

Johnson, Di. *Great Danes Today.* New York: Howell Book House, 1994.

Important Note

This book is concerned with selecting, keeping, and raising Great Danes. The publisher and the author think it is important to point out that the advice and information for the Dane's maintenance applies to healthy, normally developed animals. Anyone who acquires an adult dog or one from an animal shelter must consider that the animal may have behavioral problems and may, for example, bite without any visible provocation. Such anxiety biters are dangerous for the owner as well as the general public.

Caution is further advised in the association of children with dogs, in meetings with other dogs, and in exercising the dog without a leash—especially dogs the size of a Great Dane!

Acknowledgments

I owe much to my wife, co-writer, and partner, Cathie for her encouragement and support during the writing of this book. My son, Shawn, and his wife, Lisa, have also been of real help during this process. It is impossible to think of a grand breed like the Great Dane without envisioning one of the excellent dogs playing nursemaid to my three grandchildren; Ann Catherine, Peter Joel, and Julia.

Many thanks to Bob O'Sullivan for his patience, and to Barron's for their continued efforts in putting affordable, individually written, high-quality pet books in the hands of readers around the world.

The Great Dane is a breed of quiet dignity, great strength, keen sensitivity and extreme loyalty. On September 11, 2001, these same traits were evidenced in awesome qualities by New York's police officers, firefighters, emergency personnel, and citizens. I don't think that these memories are sullied by honoring them (and the unknown thousands of others doing the same jobs throughout the United States) by dedicating this small book about a giant breed to them.

About the Author

Joe Stahlkuppe is a widely read pet columnist, author and freelance magazine writer. A lifelong fan of purebred dogs, he has written over a dozen books, a few of them *Barron's Pet Owner Manuals*. Joe, an ordained clergyman, is also pastor of a small church in an old mining community in Alabama and is involved with a weekly pet radio show. He lives on a small farm in Jefferson County, Alabama with his wife Cathie. A pet and fundraiser consultant, he divides his time between his work and his three grandchildren—Anne Catherine, Peter, and Julia.

Photo Credits

Norvia Behling: 72. Kent and Donna Dannen: 8, 16, 24 (bottom left), 25 (top right, bottom left), 29, 32 (bottom left), 33 (top), 36 (top right, bottom), 37, 44 (top and bottom), 45 (bottom), 61, 65, 68, 88. Tara Darling: 21, 25 (top left), 32 (top right), 56, 57, 81, 89. Pets by Paulette: 2–3, 4, 5, 12, 13, 17, 24 (top, bottom right), 32 (top left, bottom right), 33 (bottom), 36 (top left), 41, 45 (top), 49, 64, 73, 76, 84, 92. Judith E. Strom: 20, 25 (bottom right), 28, 40, 52, 53 (left), 60. Connie Summers: 48, 53 (right), 69.

Cover Credits

Front cover: Barbara Augello. Back cover: Pets by Paulette. Inside front cover: Pets by Paulette. Inside back cover: Kent and Donna Dannen.

© Copyright 2002 by Barron's Educational Series, Inc. Prior edition © Copyright 1994 by Barron's Educational Series, Inc.

All inquiries should be addressed to:
Barron's Educational Series, Inc.
250 Wireless Boulevard
Hauppauge, NY 11788
www.barronseduc.com

International Standard Book No. 0-7641-1890-0

Library of Congress Catalog Card No. 2001056570

Library of Congress Cataloging-in-Publication Data
Stahlkuppe, Joe.
Great Danes : everything about purchase, care, nutrition, breeding, behavior, and training / Joe Stahlkuppe ; illustrations by Michele Earle-Bridges.
p. cm.
Includes bibliographical references (p.) and index.
ISBN 0-7641-1890-0
1. Great Dane. I. Earle-Bridges, Michele. II. Title.
SF429.G7 S73 2002
636.73—dc21   2001056570

Printed in China
9 8 7 6 5